Praise for *Placed for a Purpose*

"If you've ever had the desire to see God work in and through you right where He has you, then *Placed for a Purpose* is the perfect practical and heart-engaging guide. In the words of Rosaria Butterfield, get ready for an adventure of 'making strangers into neighbors, and neighbors into the family of God.'"

David Robbins, President and CEO of FamilyLife

"The McKinneys remind us how biblically rooted and practical 'loving your neighbor' really is and thereby inspire us to return to the 'old ways' of doing small group gospel outreach through building relational bridges with our neighbors. This excellent resource trains our church planters why and how to engage in neighboring."

    Philip Douglass, PhD, Professor Emeritus of Applied Theology, Covenant Theological Seminary; Director of Church Planting for Missouri Presbytery of the PCA

"I have no doubt that *Placed for a Purpose* will be the catalyst behind thousands of changed lives. The invitation from the McKinneys into the practice of neighboring will impact countless families and neighborhoods. The ripple effect is immeasurable. Their approach to building and strengthening community with those we live around is theologically rich but also refreshingly practical. It's easy to read, full of insight, and provides a clear—yet approachable—call to action. The McKinneys, pulling from their decades of relational ministry, show us we don't have to go far at all to make an impact on the world. There is so much potential right where we live. After reading *Placed for a Purpose*, you simply won't ever see your neighborhood the same."

    Polly Conner, Co-founder of Thriving Home; Co-author of *From Freezer to Table* & *From Freezer to Cooker*

"Chris and Elizabeth live this out in their own lives! Their approach is rich in theology and easy to apply in a multitude of different ways. When you read *Placed for a Purpose*, you will find yourself wanting to create margin in your life so you can be more present with the people who live right outside your front door. They will help you to overcome the awkwardness that many of us feel about meeting and getting to know our neighbors. They are the real deal and these tools will help you to live out the Great Commandment."

Dave Runyon, Co-author of *Art of Neighboring*

"Over the course of two years I enjoyed watching Chris and Elizabeth develop a ministry they called 'neighboring.' They both served in campus ministry for many years and had proven experience in reaching college students with the gospel. But neighboring was different in significant ways. And they had to find new ways of doing ministry that were intentionally relational and neighborly. As I watched this change as their pastor, I saw them having a lot of fun and neighbors were responding in large numbers. As Chris completed his Master of Divinity degree in seminary, he and Elizabeth were able to bring an interesting biblical theology into neighboring that has excited and equipped many others in our church to do likewise. I was so excited about what I heard that I had them present their new materials to our 70-person staff team. The material in this book is really good—insightful, educational, motivating, and actually fun to do while you make new friends and become more, well, neighborly."

Dave Cover, Co-lead Pastor, The Crossing, Columbia, Missouri

"This book could radically change the way we view and engage our neighbors. Most of us know that Jesus told us to love them—our neighbors—but we struggle to know how to do that in concrete, practical ways. Grounding us in the biblical story, Chris and Elizabeth McKinney show us what we need to know, what the posture of our heart needs to be, and the actual steps we can do to be a good neighbor. *Placed for a Purpose* will both compel and equip you to open your door, say hello, and love the people who live next door, across the street, upstairs, and in your community. May the kingdom of God be advanced in our neighborhoods as we learn what it means to truly be a good neighbor."

Courtney Doctor, Coordinator of Women's Initiatives, The Gospel Coalition; Author of *From Garden to Glory: A Bible Study on the Bible's Story*

Placed for a Purpose

foreword by Dr. Tasha Chapman

PLACED FOR A PURPOSE

A Simple and Sustainable Vision for
Loving Your Next-Door Neighbors

CHRIS AND ELIZABETH MCKINNEY

GCD Books

Placed for a Purpose:
A Simple and Sustainable Vision for Loving Your Next-Door Neighbors

© 2020 Chris and Elizabeth McKinney
All rights reserved.

GCD Books
Austin, TX

GCD Books is a ministry of Gospel-Centered Discipleship. Our purpose is to produce resources that make, mature, and multiply disciples of Jesus.

To get more resources from Gospel-Centered Discipleship, visit us at GCDiscipleship.com/Books and follow us on Twitter @GCDiscipleship.

GCD editorial: Lauren Bowerman, Alexandra Richter
Front cover design: Laura Schembre (copperstreetdesign.com)
Back cover & interior design: Benjamin Vrbicek (benjaminvrbicek.com)

Paperback ISBN: 978-0-578-73648-8
Ebook ISBN: 978-0-578-73649-5

Scripture quotations are from The ESV® Bible (The Holy Bible, English Standard Version®), copyright © 2001 by Crossway, a publishing ministry of Good News Publishers. 2016 Text Edition. Used by permission. All rights reserved.

All emphases in Scripture quotations have been added by the author.

To Nathan and Cathy,
who were there from the very beginning.

And to all our neighbors—you are our people.

CONTENTS

BY DR. TASHA CHAPMAN

ho is my neighbor? My mind first jumps to answer with Jesus's parable of the Good Samaritan. *My neighbor is any person in need, in my path, as I go about my day.* Then I remind myself, *Wait, Jesus has much more for me to learn from his answer to that question.* The word "neighbor" moves me to the more foundational question from the Great Commandment: *Am I loving my neighbors as myself?* But before I can answer, I must first ask, *Who are my neighbors, the actual people living near me?*

Daily we enter our cars in garages for long commutes and spend little free time outside in our neighborhoods. Many live in apartments and speed from our door to the bus with just a nod to others as we pass. Rarely do neighbors regularly ask each other to borrow the proverbial cup of sugar. This decline of trust and increase in isolation is palpable.

Does it matter who lives near me physically when our lives don't seem to intersect? Yes! Simply stated, it keeps us from flourishing the way God intended. Our lack of spending time with and trusting our neighbors correlates to increasingly polarized opinions and politics in society and to significant decreases in physical health and mental wellbeing. We have become fast-paced, hurried, wired, consumeristic, transient, and highly individualistic.

God makes it clear in the Bible that a true response to his sacrificial love is demonstrated by our love for God and our neighbors. "On these two commandments depend all the Law and the Prophets" (Matthew 22:37–40, ESV). This is the big picture of our Creator's plan for us. God gave us new life by faith in Jesus so that we might be salt and light, bringing blessing to the people and places in our contexts. This is good, hard work, and our culture makes it even more challenging for us to learn to love strangers and to share our hope in the gospel with them.

I am writing these words amid the COVID-19 lockdown. Three months stuck at home makes it evident that virtual time with people does not meet our need for community. Both our biblical theology and a deep sense of belonging connected to physical space inform us that human flourishing requires meaningful relationships. It was not good for Adam to be alone in the garden even though he enjoyed perfect fellowship with God there. We are embodied creatures created in the image of our Triune God; we need human contact and physical presence. We do not survive long without either. Connection to others increases our sense of purpose and meaning, positively influences our identity, and moves us to acknowledge our interdependence.

This book provides a much-needed, hope-filled, creative course for learning to be a good neighbor, literally. On a topic rarely discussed in church and long forgotten in our broader culture, these lessons meet a need in our Christian growth.

This is no ordinary small group Bible study. The McKinneys lived these lessons with their neighbors before teaching them. Then, to strengthen it further, they field tested the study with small groups living in various types of neighborhoods. Expect no dull meetings with this book: no awkward silences, no discussions merely pooling opinions, no forgetfulness between weeks. These lessons create space for meaningful learning through a variety of methods. The thoughtful questions provide the structure we need for personal reflection, careful observations of Scripture texts, hearty discussions, decisions of commitment, and prayer. The lessons connect to where we live, with stories, examples, biblical theology, and Bible passages.

For many years I have taught curriculum design and edited lesson drafts from both seminary students and seasoned ministry leaders. I am enthusiastic about how educationally and theologically rich this study is for equipping us. The McKinneys properly motivate us to learn "neighboring" through a deeper understanding of God's grace and our part in his redemptive work. Lessons engage us beyond mere information toward new attitudes and actions. The authors challenge our assumptions one step at a time about the place we call home and the people next door. Then, the end of the lesson leads us to respond to God's grace by trying something new to reach out to our neighbors.

How can we deepen our connection to the people and place where we live? What does it take to find common values on which to build bridges of trust? How can we create more peace, safety, welcome, goodness, and hope in our immediate community? This curriculum is a journey for living into the answers. It takes us step by step through small acts that can make big differences in creating healthy community and a culture of neighborliness.

Building belonging takes courage and vulnerability. It takes practice in the arts of thankfulness, truthfulness, promise keeping, and hospitality—acts that lead us to a new, wonderful way of being "at home." As we work through this book together, we can expect to see our homes expand beyond their walls. Our neighborhood will join in the blessings of feeling more comfortable, more physically and psychologically safe, and more welcomed, known, understood, and valued. As neighbors we can become co-owners and co-creators of a true community.

I am fond of the way Asbury Seminary Professor Emerita Christine Pohl calls us to pursue hospitality with joy and holy hope in her research. She summarizes it this way:

> We offer hospitality within the context of knowing Jesus as both our greater host and our potential guest. The grace we experience in receiving Jesus' welcome energizes our hospitality while it undermines our pride and self-righteousness. The possibility of welcoming Christ as our guest strengthens our kindness and fortitude in responding to strangers.[1]

Our sovereign King Jesus is full of mercy and compassion toward all people. As we learn more deeply of his love for us, may it flow out to the immediate people who live near us. I wish you a wonderful time of fellowship and growth as you create a more blessed space of belonging in the place you call home.

Tasha D. Chapman
(PhD, Trinity Evangelical Divinity School) Professor
at Covenant Theological Seminary, Co-author of
Resilient Ministry and *The Politics of Ministry*

PART I

THE BIG PICTURE OF NEIGHBORING

[KNOW]

NEIGHBORING IN GOD'S BIG REDEMPTIVE STORY

We certainly weren't looking for one more thing to do. We had just moved into a new home and were in the most stressful season of our lives. As an introvert, I (Chris) was already maxed with directing a local college ministry and commuting to seminary, so reaching out to the neighbors just wasn't on my radar. Elizabeth was sapped and barely keeping her head above water while balancing ministry responsibilities along with caring for our four young kids. Home was a place of survival mode where we hunkered down and tried to do the next urgent thing. Looking back, we were really at a crossroads. Despite the persistent pull to stay in our busy, overwhelmed, and insulated bubble and leave our neighbors alone, there began to grow in us a sense that we needed people right around us. And, we thought, maybe it could be something fun and lifegiving in the midst of our monotony. So, we threw a small fish fry. Little did we know at the time that God was pulling us out of the cultural story of neighboring and sweeping us into his story of redemption in our neighborhood.

Maybe you're like us. Maybe you're wondering how and where neighboring could possibly fit into your life. Maybe you're barely keeping afloat as it is and you're just waiting until the end of the day when you can finally have some down time. We get it. We need our homes to be places where we can rest, heal, and recharge. But what if we were to expand our belief that home is primarily a place to escape? What if we developed a mindset that home can also be a place to engage? What if God not only wants to provide healing and restoration for you at home but for your neighbors as well? And what if your neighbors are a means of grace in your life to heal and restore you?

Perhaps you're excited or cautiously optimistic about this whole neighboring thing. Maybe you've sensed that growing desire to get to know your neighbors and see God's kingdom come in your neighborhood. Wherever you are right now—whether overwhelmed, excited, or nervous—we believe God has placed you for a purpose and we want to help prepare you for the long haul of neighboring. Neighboring, after all, is much more like a crockpot than a microwave. Although microwaves are wonderful inventions, neighboring thrives in the world of marinades and slow cooking. Over time, you will get to experience the rich development of sustainable relationships that bear a lasting impact. Just think low and slow.

In order to push through the highs and lows of neighboring we must be swept up into God's story. That is what will dictate how we respond in the day in and day out with our neighbors. How we engage—or don't engage—with those who live next door is largely framed by the greater narrative in which we see ourselves.

The Cultural Narrative: Just Leave Them Alone

Although there are certainly varying subplots and subcultural narratives written into our nation's history, there seems to be a larger, overarching cultural story making its way into the fabric of our neighborhoods. As we may have observed, this narrative has shifted dramatically throughout the years. In the past, being "neighborly" was defined primarily by knowing your neighbors personally and introducing yourself to new neighbors when they moved in. Neighborliness was characterized by the understanding that one could rely on a neighbor in times of need.

We don't know when the story changed but we intuitively know it did. Now a "good neighbor" is based less on connection and more on etiquette. The good neighbor now is the one who takes the trash out properly, keeps the music down at night, and maintains peace. It's not difficult to imagine what would happen if we lived out of this kind of story brand for long. Conceivably, garage doors would remain perpetually closed, neighbors would be driven toward increased self-sufficiency, and we would feel more isolated in our homes. We'd likely hide behind our screens and even lose our ability to engage with those who might look, speak, or vote differently than us, resulting in heightened polarization and taller fences for protection. Perhaps without even realizing it, we'd feel lonelier than ever before. The message has become "Just leave them alone." And this is what we do.

The Biblical Story

In stark contrast to the cultural narrative stands the biblical story telling God's great plan of redemption. It's the story he has been writing since the beginning, a story in which he woos his followers out of the safety of their front doors into many dangers, toils, and snares. His kingdom is meant to touch every aspect of our lives, including how we interact with our neighbors. Whereas the cultural story says, "Don't make eye contact as you walk up your apartment stairwell" and "Open the garage door, pull the car in, shut the garage door," the gospel story, in contrast, calls us into our own neighborhoods to see God's story of redemption unfolding. Have you ever considered how your address fits into God's big plan? What would change if you began to live out of a better story?

Neighboring in God's Big Redemptive Story

Creation: The First Neighborhood

The first neighborhood was small—only God, Adam, and several pets and plants. It was a wonderful garden, yet God specifically said it wasn't good for "man to be alone."[1] So a third neighbor was added and there remained no gossip, no theft, no building code violations, no bad blood, no neighborly friction of any kind—just Adam, Eve, and God, relating to one another without any next-door drama.

Adam knew from the start that his need for a neighbor, Eve, was not a weakness or flaw in God's design any more than it was a weakness for the plants in the garden to need sunlight in order to live. In the same way, God has woven into our very DNA a need for people. Our need to be in relationship with others is not a result of the fall; rather, it has been God's design from the very beginning. Although God's creation of the heavens and earth was nothing short of spectacular, his crowning moment in the creative process was creating mankind in his own image. To be made in the very image of God meant, among many other things, we were created for relationship, for community, and for neighbors—not just any kind of neighbors but ones who would know and love us for who we really are. And God looked at this first neighborhood and said that it was good.

The Fall: Neighborly Discord

But as the story goes, an evil, chaos-causing enemy disguised as a serpent convinced Adam and Eve to trust in themselves rather than in God and the neighborhood fell apart. Fences were built, lines were drawn, and security cameras were installed. Their rebellion ushered in a new relational reality: isolation from both God and others. Something inside them died, and as highly relational beings hardwired for relationships, the consequences were catastrophic and eternally extensive.[2] Things really haven't improved since. We've inherited these same genes of insecurity, disdain, suspicion, and self-reliance, and these genes are felt in every cul-de-sac.

If God had said Adam would need a neighbor alongside him and that it was "not good for man to be alone" in a perfect world, how much more do you imagine he would need a neighbor in a fallen world where he'd see and experience things he was never meant to see? Death and loss would now stand relentlessly knocking at his doorstep. We need those grim visits to be followed by those of a good neighbor, but in our modern world, we put up our "No Solicitors" sign and hole up inside—just Netflix and us. We substitute face-to-face with screen-to-screen, and at first we don't seem to notice when likes and retweets leave us wanting. But when we lose a loved one, start a new job, or move to a new neighborhood, regardless of how many people we know or the breadth of our social media presence, there's a nagging pain. We feel the effects of a world cursed by sin because we feel something we were never meant to feel: loneliness.

Yet, we are somehow amazed when studies reveal that loneliness may increase our chances of premature death by fifty percent.[3] We can't help but gasp in disbelief when we hear that research shows prolonged experiences of loneliness and relational disconnect are as harmful on our long-term health as smoking and obesity[4] or that England has appointed a minister of loneliness.[5] One psychologist put it this way: "Human beings are biologically engineered for human interaction."[6] *Hmm, sounds like Genesis.* Despite all these social and scientific revelations, no neighborhood has been found immune to this loneliness pandemic. We've all got the bug and it's just one sign that confirms things aren't as they should be.

Redemption: Placed for a Purpose

Thankfully, God didn't leave us alone. With the devastating reality of Adam and Eve's decision still lingering in the air, God initiated a plan to reconcile us to himself and each other. His plan was rooted in a people and a place. God chose the family of Abraham, asked them to pack the moving van, and promised that one day, through their line, a Messiah would come. In the meantime, as their family grew, he wanted them to reflect his name, his character, and his values to their neighbors. He gave them the Law to guide their worship and everyday interactions so that their new neighborhoods would be places of peace and protection, governed by love. These instructions were given so that their neighbors would literally say, "Wow, their God seems amazing!"

The story continued and centuries later, the Messiah arrived in the person of Jesus and announced: "The Kingdom of God has come near to you."[7] He invited people to repent of their sins and become kingdom citizens, an invitation that was made possible by his impending sacrificial death and resurrection. He demonstrated that wherever the kingdom is present, restoration begins to happen in the lives of real people with real problems in real neighborhoods. He said the most important thing we could ever do was to love God and love our neighbor. Then, just before his ascension into heaven, he made it clear that the invitation into his kingdom is to be extended as we tell others about him and invite those around us to live under his rule. We do this in the limited places and local spaces in which God has placed us.

Let's put it another way. Imagine your neighborhood under a curse of an eternal winter. Temperatures remain bitterly cold, gardens go fallow, trees are barren and fruitless, and soil sleeps under a perpetual blanket of snow. No birds chattering, no butterflies migrating, no purple or yellow bulbs blooming, no trees budding, no signs of green pushing their way through the dirt, and no smell of spring—just dormancy.

In a sense, that's what has happened in your neighborhood. As part of God's big story of redemption, he created us in his image to enjoy him and each other and the world he made. But the curse of sin has come like a wintery sleep and left our hearts cold, isolated, hardened, and dead. King Jesus broke the curse at the cross. During his time on earth, he promised to one day restore his creation completely. His friends and followers saw bits of that future kingdom sprouting up as the effects of winter were undone right before their eyes. But sin and its consequences still linger in the world today. The snow is still melting.

Until the day Jesus makes all things new, he has invited us into this interim chapter in his larger story of redemption to bear his curse-cancelling image wherever we go. This means that in your little corner of your neighborhood, God desires to use ordinary people to make his kingdom flourish in your neighborhood. He is calling you to join him in pushing back against the effects of sin and death. In short, he wants to use you to bring spring to your neighborhood.

What might this actually look like? It means looking for opportunities to extend the invitation of God's kingdom to our neighbors and discerning the pace of their spiritual journey. Along with that, neighboring might mean picking up trash at times. When a neighbor's dog is lost, it means helping them search. Where there's crime, set up a neighborhood watch. Where there's a neighbor you've previously only waved to, go over and introduce yourself. Maybe it means hosting an apartment mixer, porch party, or barbeque for people in your building. Redemptive neighboring could involve planting flowers, checking on lonely neighbors, starting a community garden, or simply lingering to chat on your driveway. It's engaging neighborhood drama with grace and truth, lightening the load when we can, or helping to disentangle a neighbor when they're caught in anger. It's allowing your mind to drift to prayer for specific neighbors and any opportunity you have to weaken the effects of sin and see God's kingdom come.

And we do all this in the physical location where God has placed us. Paul reminds us that our place has been sovereignly determined by God: "He marked out their appointed times in history and the boundaries of their lands. God did this so that they would seek him and perhaps reach out for him and find him, though he is not far from any one of us."[8] Rosaria Butterfield gets it right when she says, "God doesn't get the address wrong."[9] Your address is not an accident, and neither is your neighbor's.

Restoration: Neighborhoods Made Right

As the final chapter of the biblical story unfolds, we learn that everything sad in our neighborhoods will be reversed. Revelation 21 tells us that one day all things in creation will be restored to the way they were meant to be from the beginning—including our relationship with God, each other, and every aspect of creation you can imagine. We will live in neighborhoods that function the way God intended. Can you fathom what fully restored neighborhoods might look like in the new earth? What do you think it will be like to live next to people without the destructive and isolating powers of sin at work in our lives and in the lives of our neighbors? Can you imagine living in a neighborhood with no crime? No gossip? No conflict? In these neighborhoods, people aren't lonely—they're known fully and accepted in every way. How we think about the final chapter influences the way we live in our neighborhoods now because God wants us to live with our neighbors in ways that reflect what is to come.

So, which story is currently influencing the way you show up when you walk out your front door?

When Jesus taught us to pray, "Thy kingdom come, thy will be done on earth as it is in heaven,"[10] he was demonstrating the answer to "What ought I do?" He was pushing back against a fatalistic, laissez-faire attitude that sees the brokenness and isolation and says, "It is what it is." He was intending to create in us a holy discontent that yearns for the kingdom of God to break into where we are in chapter three, the period of redemption.

You are being summoned out of the cultural narrative which says, "Just leave them alone" and into a story that might be initially intimidating to you and, because people are messy, a little thorny at times. But as you start to see God use you to usher in his kingdom in perhaps some unexpected ways, you just might begin to really believe that your address isn't an accident after all.

Discussion Guide

Purpose of the Discussion

To compare and contrast the cultural story for neighboring with God's Big Redemptive story.

Chapter Refresher

In this lesson, we compared and contrasted the cultural story of neighboring with God's Big Redemptive story. The culture tells us that a good neighbor will take the trash out, keep the noise down, and leave his or her neighbors alone. In sharp contrast to the cultural story stands the biblical story. This metanarrative can be broken into four chapters: (1) Creation: The First Neighborhood (2) The Fall: Neighborly Discord (3) Redemption: Placed for a Purpose (4) Restoration: Neighborhoods Made Right. We are currently in chapter three, placed by God in the story of redemption that is unfolding right around us in our neighborhoods.

Discussion Questions

1. **Read:** Maybe you're like us. Maybe you're wondering how and where neighboring could possibly fit into your life. Maybe you're barely keeping afloat as it is and are just waiting until the end of the day when you can finally have some down time. We get it. We need our homes to be places where we can rest, heal, and recharge.

   Perhaps you're excited or cautiously optimistic about this whole neighboring thing. Maybe you've sensed that growing desire to want to get to know your neighbors and see God's kingdom come in your neighborhood. Wherever you are right now—whether overwhelmed, excited, or nervous—we believe God has placed you for a purpose and we want to help prepare you for the long haul of neighboring.

Question: As you begin this study on neighboring are you nervous and overwhelmed or excited and cautiously optimistic? Something else? Share any obstacles that might be standing in your way.

2. **Read:** Although there are certainly varying subplots and subcultural narratives written into our nation's history, there seems to be a larger, overarching cultural story making its way into the fabric of our neighborhoods. As we may have observed, this narrative has shifted dramatically throughout the years. In the past, being "neighborly" was defined primarily by knowing your neighbors personally and introducing yourself to new neighbors when they moved in. Neighborliness was characterized by the understanding that one could rely on a neighbor in times of need.

    We don't know when the story changed but we intuitively know it did. Now a "good neighbor" is based less on connection and more on etiquette. The good neighbor now is the one who takes the trash out properly, keeps the music down at night, and maintains peace. It's not difficult to imagine what would happen if we lived out of this kind of story brand for long.

Question: Thinking about your own neighborhood context, how do you see the current cultural story that says, "Just leave them alone" affecting your neighborhood as a whole? How do you see the current cultural story affecting you individually?

3. **Read:** The first neighborhood was small—only God, Adam, and lots of pets and plants. It was a wonderful garden, yet God specifically said that it wasn't good for "man to be alone." So, Adam knew from the start that his need for a neighbor, Eve, was not a weakness or flaw in God's design any more than it was a weakness for the plants in the garden to need sunlight in order to live. In the same way, God has woven into our very DNA a need for people. Our need to be in relationship with others is not a result of the fall; rather it has been part of God's design from the very beginning.

Question: In Genesis 1 and 2 we read about how God created us to be in relationship with him and with others. Use your imagination and brainstorm how life in a neighborhood like yours would have looked if sin had never entered the world.

4. **Read:** But as the story goes, an evil, chaos-causing enemy disguised as a serpent convinced Adam and Eve to trust in themselves rather than in God and the neighborhood fell apart. Fences were built, lines were drawn, and security cameras were installed. Their

rebellion ushered in a new relational reality: disconnect and isolation from both God and others. Something inside them died, and as highly relational beings hardwired for relationships, the consequences were catastrophic and eternally extensive. Things really haven't improved since. We've inherited these same genes of insecurity, disdain, suspicion, and self-reliance and these genes are felt in every cul-de-sac.

Question: How do you see the effects of sin and brokenness in your neighborhood? How do you experience disorder, discord, or disconnect?

5. **Read:** Paul reminds us that our place has been sovereignly determined by God: "He marked out their appointed times in history and the boundaries of their lands. God did this so that they would seek him and perhaps reach out for him and find him, though he is not far from any one of us."[11] Rosaria Butterfield gets it right when she says, "God doesn't get the address wrong."[12] Your address is not an accident, and neither is your neighbor's.

Question: What is the story behind how you ended up in your current neighborhood? How might God have been at work behind the scenes to place you there? How does that change the way you see your neighbors and your role in the neighborhood?

6. **Read:** As the final chapter of the biblical story unfolds, we learn that everything sad in our neighborhoods will be reversed. How

we think about the final chapter influences the way we live in our neighborhoods now because God wants us to live with our neighbors in ways that reflect what is to come.

Question: What would change today in your neighborhood if everything sad were to become untrue? What might change physically? What prejudices would be wiped out? What fears would be eliminated? What does it evoke in you to think about your neighbors and neighborhood being fully healed and restored?

Assignment

Sometimes we forget that big things can happen through small steps. Discuss one small step you want to take this week to show God's love to a neighbor.

Neighboring Prayer for the Week

Lord, thank you for inviting and bringing me into your story of redemption. I know you are at work in my neighborhood and you have placed me for a purpose. Please guide my interactions with my neighbors and make them fruitful.

BRINGING THE GREAT COMMANDMENT HOME

It's Okay; It's the Neighbors

On February 14, 2018, Scot Peterson was sitting in his office at Stoneman Douglas High School in Parkland, Florida when he heard a report come over his radio that fireworks had possibly been set off on school property. Longtime deputy and security officer, Scot walked and then began running toward the location of the incident. When he arrived on the scene, he radioed another police officer: "Shots have been fired inside Building 1200!" Footage revealed that rather than entering and confronting the gunman, he remained outside with his handgun drawn, walking almost aimlessly for the remaining three minutes that seventeen students and faculty were shot dead.

In the days that followed, parents accused Peterson of letting innocent people die. The President described him as a "coward" and his former boss called him a "disgrace and an awful human." News reporters and angry community members crowded around his home, forcing him to withdraw and close the curtains. "What now?" asked Scot's exasperated girlfriend, Lydia, as the motion detector on their front porch went off and she peeked out the window. From the background, Scot murmured, "Tell them I'm not home." "It's okay," said Lydia, "It's the neighbors . . . Jim and Kelly."[1]

Who were some of the only people to come and check on this man in the weeks and months that followed the attack? *The neighbors.* The only ones with true access to this hurting soul pushed through angry crowds and risked condemnation to help someone many deemed unworthy of compassion. And on this particular occasion, they brought cookies.

I don't know about you, but reading the phrase "It's the neighbors" was not what I was expecting. This story is surprising and powerful because Jim and Kelly went against the cultural current of neighborly isolation and didn't simply leave their neighbors alone. They had been placed in close proximity to a guy who was experiencing some of the darkest days of his life and instead of "hoping for the best" for him, they took the opportunity to be real neighbors. In many ways, that's exactly what Jesus wants us to do. Jesus highlights this in Luke 10. Let's read, starting in verse 25:

And behold, a lawyer stood up to put him to the test, saying, "Teacher, what shall I do to inherit eternal life?" He said to him, "What is written in the Law? How do you read it?" And he answered, "You shall love the Lord your God with all your heart and with all your soul and with all your strength and with all your mind, and your neighbor as yourself." And he said to him, "You have answered correctly; do this, and you will live."[2]

The Non-Neighbor

Some of you might be having underlying anxiety or an inner objection. *Woah, woah, woah. Are you saying when Jesus said to "love your neighbor" he meant my literal next-door neighbor? Because I'm pretty sure "neighbor" is defined more broadly.* You're right, it is. A neighbor can be anyone who is close by to us. Yet, is it possible that we can get caught in such broad generalities thinking about the neighbors "out there" that we forget about our neighbors "right here"? Perhaps what comes to mind when we hear the word "neighbor" is more selective than we care to admit. Stop and think about it for a second. When you hear Jesus's words to "love your neighbor as yourself," whose faces come to mind? Maybe, when pressed, we conveniently find ourselves drawn to see our neighbors as those we presently know and love. Our answer to the question "Who is my neighbor?" reveals what we love, what we fear, and where we draw our lines.

Read Luke 10:29–37

We know very little about this guy, but a few things we do know: (1) He's very religious. When we hear the word lawyer, we need to think expert in the Mosaic law. He's more of an Old Testament scholar. (2) Whatever his motive for doing so, he's trying to "test" Jesus. (3) He desires to justify himself.

Jesus's response to the religious man is to tell a story about two more religious guys. Unfortunately, the two saint-like men aren't so saintly after all. They come across a beaten man and both pass by to the other side of the cul-de-sac. You're left to wonder, *Are all the people in this neighborhood so hardhearted (or just the churchgoers)?* In a plot twist that would have jarred Jesus's audience, along comes a Samaritan, a racially-mixed Jew considered a second-class citizen by those around him. He stops with oil and wine, lavishly gives of his time and money, and takes the man to a place where he can get the healing he needs.

We can't help but scratch our chins as we picture how this expert in the law would have received this story. Isn't it kind of fascinating to imagine him standing there trying to pull one over on Jesus with all the right questions: "What must I do to inherit eternal life?" and "Who is my neighbor?" Yet, the poor guy didn't know that 2,000 years later we'd still be reading about what was beneath the surface of his heart. "Desiring to justify himself," he asked Jesus, "Who is my neighbor?" Turns out, he might have already had an answer in mind for both questions. He thought they were rhetorical questions and could probably have answered them for Jesus: "I'm a good kid. I volunteer at the food bank, give money to the homeless guy downtown, take meals to friends when they have a baby or are in crisis. Just give me the neighboring manual, because I'm pretty sure I got this."

We know he asked the question to justify himself. Why else may he have asked? There were a million other responses he could have had upon thinking through the words "Love your neighbor," but he deliberately asks, "And *who* is my neighbor?"[3] David Garland in his commentary on the book of Luke says,

> The lawyer wants to know how and where to draw the line. What can be demanded of me? Whom exactly am I required to love? The question implies that there can be a non-neighbor!

The lawyer also wants to know from whom he can safely withhold his love.[4]

We're like this lawyer too. We think we need to draw the lines somewhere; we're limited humans for goodness' sake. We need to determine (with God's blessing of course) whom exactly we are required to love. And maybe it's not entirely bad that he wanted to safely withhold love from those who didn't make the list; it's a rough world out there, right? Like this Old Testament scholar, we have better neighbors in mind. Is it possible, for example, that with all the wonderful benefits of being connected virtually, we have moved on from our geographic neighbors to more exciting ones who may just happen to like a lot of the same things we do? Is it possible that our next-door neighbors have become our *non-neighbors?*

If they don't look like us, talk like us, go to our church, or see things from our political point of view, we check out. Whether you live on a block that is racially homogeneous or not, we find a thousand ways to separate ourselves and look for our people, our tribe. Like the priest and the Levite, we sometimes walk—or drive—around these non-neighbors to the other side of the street. In the end, a neighbor can be defined as much more than the people who live next door, but it can never be defined as less.

Proving to be a Neighbor

When Jesus finished telling the story, he turned to the lawyer and asked, "Which of these three, do you think, proved to be a neighbor to the man who fell among the robbers?" He answered, "The one who showed him mercy." Jesus affirmed his answer and said, "You go, and do likewise."[5] When Jesus asked which of the three *proved* to be a neighbor, he was asking which of the three demonstrated neighborly love with their actions.

Did you notice how Jesus flipped the script? When the Bible expert asks, "Who is my neighbor?" Jesus responds with a different and better question: "Which of these three proved to be a neighbor?" The first question points outward, placing the emphasis on who was worthy of receiving help—who's in and who's out? The second question points inward, placing the emphasis on both the heart and actions of the one doing the neighboring. When the neighbor is considered "Other," we presume a place of superiority, asking, "Who gets to be my neighbor?" When the emphasis is placed on our own hearts, we assume a sense of humble responsibility. We ask ourselves, "Is there evidence in my life that I'm truly a neighbor to those around me? If not, how can I become one?" Jesus is essentially saying, "*Be* a neighbor to others rather than ask who is worthy to be yours."

This story actually reminds me of dating, oddly enough. My wife and I worked in college ministry for many years and used to give a presentation called "Dating by Faith." There would always be a buzz in the air and students would come excited to hear what they should be looking for in a future spouse. Rather than give them a checklist of twenty desirable qualities for the other person, we encouraged them that dating was more about what God was doing in their life—less about finding the one and more about becoming the one. Jesus says we've got it all wrong. The question isn't "Who is—or isn't—my neighbor?" The question is "How will *I* demonstrate neighborly love and thus prove to be a neighbor?"

The priest and the Levite missed an opportunity to be neighbors to someone in need, to show mercy through a present, active faith. We understand though, don't we? We can imagine some of the reasons the priest and Levite failed. Maybe they were in a hurry to meet a deadline; maybe they were tired from a long day and just wanted to get home; or maybe they had assumptions about what happened to the man and didn't want to get involved. Whatever their excuses were, we can relate because ours are similar.

We pull out our phone as we walk up the stairs to our apartment just in case we run into that person with the barking dog who lives a few doors down from us. We quickly enter the garage and close the door so that we won't have to stop and say "Hi" to the neighbors getting their mail. We avoid eye contact with the neighbor we've met several times because we're too embarrassed to ask them their name again. We keep conversation at a surface level with our neighbors because we are overwhelmed by the thought of not being able to immediately get inside and unwind. And we keep walking around our neighbors and leaving them alone, just like the cultural narrative tells us to.

The Samaritan proved to be a neighbor when he set his excuses aside and stopped to bandage the man on the road. Jim and Kelly proved to be neighbors when they stopped by with cookies on Scot's porch. You can prove to be a neighbor when you introduce yourself to those next door and remember to use their names when you see them again. According to Jesus, we can't just say we're neighbors; we need to prove it.

Bringing it Home

So, is that all this story is about? This Bible teacher wants to feel good about himself, so Jesus turns the tables on him and gives an example for how to do better? If we know our Savior, we know that he has so much more in store for us than a moral heart check and a how-to. We want the neighboring manual, the example story, so that we can move on and be the hero. But Jesus doesn't offer us our own goodness. Jesus offers himself to those who have been left for dead in the ditch. And that is where we were. God has called us to good works—to show his mercy to a broken, hurting world—*and* we never grow past our need as those who were raised from the ditch by the only "Good Samaritan."

When we reduce the parable of the Good Samaritan to an example story, we remove the heartbeat of what it means to prove to be a neighbor. In order to become a neighbor to those around us, we need a heart change that only comes from embracing and experiencing the gospel. We show mercy because we have been shown mercy. We love because he first loved us—not from a place of vain superiority but of humble gratitude and responsibility. The power to love our neighbors isn't found in the command to do so, but instead it is found in Jesus.

We say with John Newton in his hymn "The Good Samaritan,"

Gently he raised me from the ground,
Pressed me to lean upon his arm;
And into every gaping wound
He poured his own all-healing balm.[6]

This week, as you pull into your neighborhood or apartment complex, let your thoughts drift toward God's love for you. Why not say a simple prayer such as, "God, please help me love the people in my neighborhood the way you have loved me. Remind me that these next-door neighbors are real people with real hurts and that you love them. Help me prove to be a neighbor to them." As you go throughout your week, look for ways to bring the Great Commandment home. Look for opportunities to stop, put away excuses and fears, and seek to take one next step in becoming a neighbor.

Discussion Guide

Purpose of the Discussion

Identify one non-neighbor and one simple way you could demonstrate love to him or her.

Chapter Refresher

In the second lesson, we look at the story of the Good Samaritan. When we ask the question "Who is—or isn't—my neighbor?" we categorize who we will or won't love. But Jesus flips the script and instead asks, "Which of these three, do you think, *proved to be a neighbor*?" (Luke 10:36). In doing so, he moves from asking, "Who's in and who's out?" to "Am I becoming a person who demonstrates love to the neighbors God has placed around me?" In other words, am I truly a neighbor to my neighbors?

Discussion Questions

1. **Question:** What reaction do you have when you hear Jim and Kelly's story? Do you find it compelling? Surprising? Why?

2. **Read:** David Garland writes, "The lawyer wants to know how and where to draw the line. What can be demanded of me? Whom exactly am I required to love? The question implies that there can be a non-neighbor! The lawyer also wants to know from whom he can safely withhold his love."[7]

   Question: We sometimes consciously or subconsciously tend to categorize people to determine who makes the list when Jesus says, "Love your neighbor." Thinking about your neighboring context, who is one neighbor that tends to fall into the non-neighbor category for you and why?

3. **Read:** The priest and the Levite missed an opportunity to become neighbors to someone in need, to show mercy through a present, active faith. We understand though, don't we? We can imagine some of the reasons the priest and Levite failed. Maybe they were in a hurry to meet a deadline; maybe they were tired from a long day and just wanted to get home; or maybe they had assumptions about what had happened to the man and didn't want to get involved. Whatever their excuses were, we can relate because ours are similar.

   Question: What are some of our excuses—whether valid or invalid—for not stopping to be a neighbor?

4. **Read:** When we reduce the parable of the Good Samaritan to an example story, we remove the heartbeat of what it means to prove to be a neighbor. In order to become a neighbor to those around us, we need a heart change that only comes from embracing and experiencing the gospel. We show mercy because we have been shown mercy. We love because he first loved us—not from a place of vain superiority but of humble gratitude and responsibility. The power to love our neighbors isn't found in the command to do so, but instead it is found in Jesus.

Question: Many of us read the parable of the Good Samaritan merely as an example story. How does it help us to identify with the person in the ditch, and how does it motivate us to show neighborly love when we see Jesus as the true Good Samaritan?

Assignment

This week, remember you once were the one in the ditch who Jesus stopped to rescue. Share one way you will practice love toward someone you've previously seen as a non-neighbor. Maybe you stop to say "Hi" and introduce yourself. Maybe you pray for them every morning when you drive by their house. Allow God to guide you to a practical step for the week.

Neighboring Prayer for the Week

God, please help me love the people in my neighborhood the way you have loved me. Remind me that these next-door neighbors are real people with real hurts and that you love them. Help me become a neighbor to them.

SEEING YOUR NEIGHBOR

In our previous lesson, we saw Jesus respond to the man asking, "Who is my neighbor?" with a challenge to become a person who demonstrates love to those we may consider *non-neighbors*. After all, the most important thing you could do in your life is love God and love your neighbor.

But sometimes, whether consciously or subconsciously, we have what we'll call "invisible neighbors." These are the people who live right around us who we don't see at all. We live in a culture where we scurry into our homes or up our apartment stairwells, hiding behind our phones, anxiously hoping to avoid neighborly interaction. It's hard to love your neighbor if you don't see your neighbor.

Mr. Rogers' Neighborhood

Ten-year-old Jeff Erlanger is seated in his wheelchair at the front porch of Mr. Rogers' Neighborhood. It is clear Mr. Rogers is expecting him and he squats down quite comfortably on the step just off the ground. He stays in this position for the entirety of their chat, and though it's only five minutes, it feels from Mr. Rogers' unhurried posture that he has all day. Mr. Rogers hangs on Jeff's every word as he shares about the surgery that left him paralyzed at seven months of age. He talks about his spinal tumor, his doctors, his bladder, and another recent surgery. After all of this, Mr. Rogers asks if he's familiar with his song "It's You I Like" because he'd like to sing it to him and with him.[1]

A child who may have been otherwise overlooked is delighted in and seen. What a beautiful picture of the Great Commandment coming alive at home, right in the neighborhood. With an unhurried attentiveness, Mr. Rogers sees Jeff. He sees the good parts and the painful ones and accepts all of him by saying, "I like you." He offered this young ten-year-old—and every viewer along with him—an unconditional *like*.

Why does a clip like this move us? What is it about being seen and accepted that touches us in such a profound way? We long to be loved like this, yet there is a part of us that says it's too good to be true. *But it is true.* Immanuel is unhurried and sitting on your porch step, bending to meet your gaze and hear your thoughts. It's you he likes.

But how can we be sure? Thankfully, we have the New Testament highlight reel with passages like Matthew 9, where we can watch Jesus in action as he demonstrated what it looked like to see and accept his neighbors.

He Came to His Own City

In the first verse of Matthew chapter 9, Jesus comes to Capernaum, "And getting into a boat he crossed over and *came to his own city*." Matthew 4:13–17 says, "And leaving Nazareth he went and *lived in Capernaum by the sea*, in the territory of Zebulun and Naphtali." Similarly, in Mark 2:1 we read, "A few days later, when Jesus again entered Capernaum, the people heard that *he had come home*."

Though Jesus traveled quite a bit during his ministry years, we see that our Lord also had a place where he came home to rest, recharge, and continue doing ministry—and that home was Capernaum.[2]

Aside from several strategic reasons why Jesus might have chosen Capernaum as a home base, an obvious reason was the fact that Peter, Andrew, James, and John were all from Capernaum. Additionally, Peter's house—likely a small insula similar to a modern-day apartment complex where multiple families shared walls with one another—was about 100 yards from the synagogue.

So, when Matthew says that Jesus came home to Capernaum, did he come home to his own house? Did he stay with Peter? We don't know exactly, but we do know that this was home during those several years.

Why is it important to imagine where Jesus slept and woke up during these stays? Because Jesus wasn't some caricature floating outside of a local context. He was an actual person who would come back somewhere to sleep at night and bump into people when he was headed out in the morning. He shared an actual wall with actual people . . . actual neighbors.

Jesus had the neighbors who did *that thing*. They had a loud party and played their music all night so he couldn't sleep. They didn't clean up after their dog. And that one family that's a little showy and pretentious—the ones that smile all phony from afar? Jesus knew them, too. The one who would never make eye contact and never wave back? Yep, he encountered them often.

As we read Matthew 9, we want you to picture Jesus as he's walking through the streets of Capernaum. When he stopped to talk and heal, there were faces he probably recognized. When he looked out on the crowds, he was seeing neighbors, with some of whom he maybe even shared a wall.

Jesus Saw His Neighbors

Repeatedly throughout this chapter—eight times to be exact—Matthew mentions Jesus seeing people. Also not coincidentally, it's in this chapter that he tells the story of Jesus restoring sight to two blind men. Matthew 9 teaches us what it means to see Jesus and be seen by him.

Read Matthew 9:1–9

Let's walk through the passage together and make a note each time Matthew records Jesus seeing someone.

Stop and read verse 1 aloud again. *He came to his own city.* We saw this already; Jesus is home. He's walking throughout the city, surrounding towns, and villages. He's going into homes. He's neighboring. In verse 2, four men[3] carry their paralytic friend to Jesus who *saw their faith.* He saw their hope, their trust, their persistence. He saw it all.

Later in verse 9, Jesus saw a man named Matthew sitting at his tax collector's booth.

Immediately following, Jesus goes to his house for dinner. This guy who's on the wrong side of politics is now hosting Jesus. And we can't help but wonder what emotions were running through him as he wrote verse 9 about himself—*Jesus saw a man named Matthew.*

Think about it. Matthew is essentially saying, "Jesus saw . . . me." Insert yourself in the story here and imagine it this way. If I had written the *Gospel*

According to Elizabeth and then said, "And he *saw* Elizabeth," what would those words have meant to me? To you? What did they mean to Matthew?

We know to some extent what they meant when we read the second part of verse 9: "He rose and followed him." We know that Matthew's life was changed forever, so much so that he wrote the very book we now hold in our hands called Matthew.

Read 9:18–25

Jairus,[4] the leader from the local synagogue, had just lost his daughter and comes to Jesus, begging him to come to his house and heal her.

Along the way, a woman who has been bleeding for twelve years stops him. Rather than moving to the other side of the road, he proved to be her neighbor when he turned around and . . . *saw her.* The woman no one saw, Jesus saw.

After healing her, Jesus arrived at Jairus's home and *he saw the flute players.* It was common in those days to hire flute players as a sign of mourning. They were likely playing songs of sorrow as people gathered to lament that this young one had died too soon. (And as a side-note, doesn't it make you wonder what the songs sounded like after Jesus raised her from the dead?) Matthew didn't need to mention the flute players at all. Mark and Luke don't mention them in their accounts. But Matthew noticed that Jesus noticed. He *saw* the flute players.

Read 9:35–36

Jesus went throughout all the towns and villages. Again, he's in their homes, at their dinner tables, in their apartment complexes—he's in their neighbor-hood.

He's seen the faith of the four friends, he's seen Matthew, he's seen the bleeding woman, he's seen the flute players, and now in verse 36 he sees the crowds: "When *he saw the crowds,* he had compassion for them, because they were harassed and helpless, like sheep without a shepherd."[5]

When we see a crowd, what do we see? I think many of us see a mob, something we need to get away from. Crowds can make us feel anxious or over-whelmed. But is that what Jesus saw? When it says, he *saw* the crowd? He saw *them.* He saw neighbors.

He saw past their exterior and into their true spir-itual condition. He saw them as sheep without a shepherd. He didn't buy into the lie that they had it all together. He didn't judge them, nor did he see a bunch of faceless nobodies, nor see past them all to-gether. He saw them as they truly were, neighbors made in the image of God yet broken because of the fall.

Warped Mirrors and Glorious Ruins

When we walk through the streets of our own Caper-naum, the way we see our neighbors is shaped by our understanding of who they are and how they were created. Jesus saw people through the lens of the *imago Dei*, which means we are created in the image of God. This was Jesus's backdrop for every personal interaction.

Genesis 1:26–27 tells us we were all created in God's image. Every believer and non-believer alike has been endowed by their Creator with his stamp, the *imago Dei*. That means every single person in your neighborhood has been marked by the very finger-print of God, made as a mirror to image him on earth. Though the mirror is warped and marred, there remains in your unbelieving neighbor the imprint of God himself.

Picture the ruins of an ancient church. You can imagine the glory for which it was created, and yet the years of disrepair remind us that things are not the way they ought to be. We're a lot like that. Theologian and author Francis Schaeffer referred to us affectionately as "glorious ruins."[6]

When we forget that our neighbors are glorious ruins, it is easy to do one of three things:

When we see only glory, we envy them.
When we see only ruin, we judge them.
When we don't see them at all, we ignore them.

What do you see when you see your neighbors? What comes to mind? It's difficult to think of anything but that *one annoying thing*. You dislike the unfriendly vibe you get when they won't make eye contact. You're tired of hearing them fight through your shared wall or parking in front of your mailbox or refusing to clean up their dog poop or their dog barking all night. Maybe they installed their fence on your property or don't take care of their yard. Have you ever found yourself pigeonholing them based on *that thing*? It's hard to do the work of finding common ground with someone when all we can think about is how they pull in with the other candidate's bumper sticker on their car. They're the non-neighbor.

Or maybe you live next to the Joneses. You only see one version of them, the smiling one. They're sort of charming and busy, but in a good way. They always seem to have a leg up, whether it's economically or socially or anything else. You wouldn't think to have compassion on them; you're too busy admiring their betterness. It's hard to see their shortcomings because there's a certain pretense and projected image that tells you they're just fine. Whether it's the image they want you to see or the image you choose to see, you believe it.

Or do you see them at all? When you pull into your neighborhood, do you see the buildings but see past the people? Are your neighbors fairly uninteresting to you? Are they faceless? Do you find that you sometimes disconnect from the fact that they are real people with real stories, real sins, and real hurts? Do they feel anonymous and remote even though they live a few feet away?

Think about it for a second. If Jesus had seen only glory when he saw the people in Matthew 9, he wouldn't have seen their need for compassion and healing. Further, if he had seen only ruin, he wouldn't have bothered healing them at all. But he saw more. He saw image bearers worthy of love but with great need. He saw Jeff Erlangers. Your neighbor has God-given strengths and gifts. Likewise, they are beset with weaknesses that mar the *imago Dei* in them. Across that fence, your neighbor carries with him both that glory and ruin—a glory which motivates our respect and a ruin which motivates our compassion.

The Neighboring Grid

As we think about what it means to have respect and compassion for our neighbors while seeing both their glory and ruin, let's look at the Neighboring Grid. As the arrow moves right, we see more glory in our neighbors; as the arrow moves up, we see more ruin. Where we see neither glory nor ruin, neighbors are invisible to us.

On the next page, read through each quadrant of the Neighboring Grid, starting with Judgment and moving counter-clockwise. As you read aloud, try to mentally identify someone in the following categories: Non-neighbors, Instagram Neighbors, and Invisible Neighbors.

Tim Keller says, "To be loved but not known is comforting but superficial. To be known and not loved is our greatest fear. But to be fully known and truly loved is, well, a lot like being loved by God. It is what we need more than anything. It liberates us from pretense, humbles us out of our self-righteousness, and fortifies us for any difficulty life can throw at us."[7] The paralytic, Matthew, the bleeding woman, the flute players, the crowds—they all experienced what it was like to be pulled out of their isolation, seen as glorious ruins, yet fully loved. Jesus saw their glory, he saw their ruin, and he had compassion. That is what it means to be fully known and truly loved. That is what it means to be seen by Jesus.

Perhaps the episode with Jeff Erlanger in Mr. Rogers' Neighborhood is so powerful because we all long to be fully known and truly loved. We can't help but marvel at the kind hero stopping to treasure this child. We have a hard time believing we're lovable, let alone likeable. And yet there he is—stopping, crouching down on that bottom step, looking you in the eyes and seeing the real you . . . accepting the real you. When you experience what it's like to be seen in this way, it may just move you out of the cultural narrative. It might move you from leaving your neighbor alone to looking into their eyes, perhaps for the first

The Neighboring Grid[8]

Judgement	Neighbors Seen as Glorious Ruins
<ul><li>We primarily see ruin so we judge them</li><li>General feelings of suspicion</li><li>No grace for mistakes</li><li>Difficult to find common ground</li><li>Walls are built to keep "us" from "them"</li><li>Non-Neighbors</li></ul>	<ul><li>We see both glory from the image of God, which motivates our respect, and ruin from the effects of sin, which motivates our compassion</li><li>Faces and names are known</li><li>Freedom to disagree and still be in relationship</li><li>Endures the messiness that comes from being in relationships</li><li>God's love experienced</li><li>See ourselves and our neighbors as Glorious Ruins</li></ul>
Isolation	**Envy**
<ul><li>We see past people so we ignore them</li><li>People are faceless & anonymous</li><li>Phones keep people distracted, busy, and isolated</li><li>We feel alone, unknown & disconnected</li><li>Invisible neighbors</li></ul>	<ul><li>We primarily see glory so we envy them</li><li>Easily fooled by an Instagram version of others, the "got it all together" version</li><li>Superficial connections</li><li>People are seen but remain hidden because they aren't truly known</li><li>Keeping up with The Joneses</li><li>Instagram Neighbors</li></ul>

time. You may begin to demonstrate, "It's you I like. It's you Jesus likes."

Isn't that what happened to Matthew? When Matthew says, "Jesus saw a man named Matthew," he's also sharing his own turning point: "Matthew saw a man named Jesus." And when you begin to see your neighbors the way Jesus sees them, some will say it was your love that led them to say the words, "Jesus saw me. And now I see Jesus."

Discussion Guide

Purpose of the Discussion

Discuss how we can move from envying, judging, or ignoring our neighbors to loving them and seeing them as "glorious ruins."

Chapter Refresher

Reading through Matthew 9, we observe Jesus interacting with his hometown Capernaum neighbors. Rather than passing by, he allows himself to be interrupted and truly see the people on his path. When he sees them, he sees the good (glory) and the bad (ruin) and he has compassion on them. When we forget that our neighbors are glorious ruins, it is easy to do one of three things: When we see only glory, we envy them. When we see only ruin, we judge them. When we don't see them at all, we ignore them. Jesus saw his neighbors as they truly were, made in the image of God, yet broken because of the fall.

Discussion Questions

1. **Read:** In the first verse of Matthew chapter 9, Jesus comes to Capernaum, "And getting into a boat he crossed over and *came to his own city*." Matthew 4:13–17 says, "And leaving Nazareth he went and *lived in Capernaum by the sea*, in the territory of Zebulun and Naphtali." Similarly, in Mark 2:1 we read, "A few days later, when Jesus again entered Capernaum, the people heard that *he had come home*." Though Jesus traveled quite a bit during his ministry years, we see that our Lord also had a place where he

came home to rest, recharge, and continue doing ministry—and that home was Capernaum.

Question: The people we see interacting with Jesus throughout this chapter were people he potentially saw on a daily basis when he was living in Capernaum. What is your reaction to knowing these were not just random people with whom Jesus had interactions? How can this thought influence the way we see and feel toward our own neighbors?

2. **Read:** Look back over the following passages in Matthew 9:

> 9:2 (Jesus saw the faith of the paralytic's friends)
>
> 9:9 (Jesus saw a tax collector named Matthew)
>
> 9:22 (Jesus saw a woman who had been sick)
>
> 9:23 (Jesus saw the flute players)
>
> 9:36 (Jesus saw the crowds)

Question: Which interaction stands out to you the most and why?

3. **Read:** Genesis 1:26–27 tells us we were all created in God's image. Every believer and non-believer alike has been endowed by their Creator with his stamp, the *imago Dei*. That means every single person in your neighborhood has been marked by the very

fingerprint of God, made as a mirror to image him on earth. Though the mirror is warped and marred, there remains in your unbelieving neighbor the imprint of God himself.

Picture the ruins of an ancient church. You can imagine the glory for which it was created, and yet the years of disrepair remind us that things are not the way they ought to be. We're a lot like that. Theologian and author Francis Schaeffer summarized it this way: "We are Glorious Ruins, that is what we are."

Question: The way Mr. Rogers saw people was shaped undoubtedly by his view of the *imago Dei*. How can a correct understanding of the *imago Dei* shift our view and feelings toward our neighbors?

4. **Read:** Look back and review the Neighboring Grid as a group.

    Question: Think about Matthew, Jairus, and the bleeding woman in regard to the Neighboring Grid. Speculate which quadrant each of them could fit in and what it might have meant to them, given their societal place in Capernaum, to been seen by Jesus.

    Question: From which quadrant do you tend to operate when it comes to relating to your neighbors? In other words, when you see these particular neighbors, do you tend to see more glory (bottom right quadrant) or more ruin (upper left quadrant)? Or do you see past people altogether (bottom left quadrant)? What's one step you could take to move toward the upper right quadrant?

5. **Read:** Your neighbor has God-given strengths and gifts. Likewise, they are beset with weaknesses that mar the *imago Dei* in them. Across that fence, your neighbor carries with him both that glory and ruin—a glory which motivates our respect and a ruin which motivates our compassion.

Question: What ruin have you observed in your neighbor's life that might motivate compassion? What glimpses have you had of the *imago Dei* that could motivate your respect?

Assignment

Plan a time as a group or individually to watch the Fred Rogers documentary *Won't You Be My Neighbor* and spend time discussing it as a group.

Neighboring Prayer for the Week

Lord, sometimes I don't even see my neighbors. If I do, I often either judge them or envy them. Please open my eyes to see that my neighbors are made in your image. Help me have both respect and compassion for them.

PART II

THE POSTURE OF NEIGHBORING

[BE]

HOSPITALITY:
WELCOME AND BE WELCOMED

Bringing the Outsider In

T he transition from fifth to sixth grade was a rough one for me (Elizabeth). In the fifth grade, I was happily oblivious to the world of cliques and social distinctions that awaited me in middle school. Who knew my ultra-short and flat, feathery haircut, very large red glasses, braces, and lack of fashion sense would be seen as a less-than-winning combination? I was clueless until I wasn't, and it was a rude awakening when I realized I was on the outside looking in.

One year later, things shifted when I met Mya. She was the queen bee over our class and had the ability to control social strings I didn't even know existed. Part of her allure was her seeming disinterest in doing what was expected to fit in. She stepped over social and ethnic lines and ran with jocks, skaters, mean girls, nerds, and drifters. And for whatever reason, Mya befriended me. She brought me in. As a result, my social life took a turn and I no longer had to experience the painful isolation that comes with being the outsider.

You might think from that point on I worked hard to include those who were excluded—that I had a sensitivity toward those on the hem. You might think I'd be careful to remember the floaters and fringers. You might . . . but you'd be wrong. Instead of having to focus my attention on *getting* in, I simply redirected it toward *staying* in.

Sadly, I still do this in some ways today.

Instead of making room at my table for the newcomer, the stranger, and the outlier, I press on in survival mode to take care of me and mine. I'm guessing I'm not the only one who tends to make sure my own needs are met while tuning out the lives around me. Many of us may think about our self-serving default settings when at work, church, or social surroundings, but what about at home with our neighbors? We talked earlier about our inclination to see the home primarily as a place to rest, retreat, and recharge— and it should be that. But what if there's more? What if there's a greater purpose to our home than simply getting our own needs met? What if God wants to mercifully lift our eyes from our own myopic tendencies? What if the stranger next door is a mercy of God to accomplish that very thing in your life?

This isn't a new idea. From the very beginning, God has revealed himself as a loving Father who delights in blessing his children. But he doesn't bless us so that we can go on living for ourselves. We are blessed in order to be a blessing.[1] We are called out of lives of self-preoccupation and into a life of hospitality. Second Corinthians 5:15 states, "And he died for all, that those who live should no longer live for themselves but for him who died for them and was raised again."

So, what do you think it means to live a life of hospitality? Depending on our upbringing, we could all provide different lists of what the word hospitable means to us. We might think of someone who is a good cook or has a well-decorated home. Maybe we think of someone who can host a great party or is generous or who provides a warm environment where others feel at home. While all of these are good, they provide an incomplete picture when it comes to understanding the heart behind biblical hospitality. As with our definition of what it means to be a good neighbor, sometimes our view of hospitality has been more shaped by the culture than the Bible. In the wise words of Inigo Montoya: "You keep using that word; I do not think it means what you think it means."[2]

Defining Hospitality

Whereas we might prefer to think of hospitality as merely the entertaining of our family and friends, the biblical writers clearly wanted us to widen our definition. Quite literally, the biblical concept of hospitality is simply to welcome and love the stranger.

The heartbeat of hospitality is one of love, expressed through a welcoming presence that receives and makes room for the outsider. It says, "Don't forget how you yourself were on the outside. Remember how you were excluded from the Covenant, how you used to not belong? Now that you're in, now that you're near, don't forget about those who still aren't at the table. Remember those who are missing."

It's hard to think about Christian hospitality without thinking of this welcome from God himself. We begin to see God as our gracious and generous host and see ourselves as his guests. We remember that though we were once strangers, he sought us, welcomed us to himself, hosted us in the wilderness, and provided for all our needs. We hear ourselves saying with the Psalmist, "You prepare a table for me."[3]

Paul says it this way to the Ephesians: "Remember that you were at that time separated from Christ, alienated from the commonwealth of Israel and strangers to the covenants of promise, having no hope and without God in the world. But now in Christ Jesus you who once were far off have been brought near by the blood of Christ."[4]

The problem is that we don't remember.

A History of Hospitality

Our Bibles remind us that the people of God are called to a rich tradition of hospitality. In the first few books of the Bible, God's people found themselves enslaved as foreigners in Egypt. As we know, they were mistreated and misplaced for hundreds of years and longed for God to rescue them from their vulnerable state. Finally, in a miraculous series of events, God delivered them out of Egypt and set them on their journey to their new home. But he instructed them along the way, "When a stranger sojourns with you in your land, you shall not do him wrong. You shall treat the stranger who sojourns with you as the native among you, and you shall love him as yourself, for you were strangers in the land of Egypt: I am the LORD your God."[5]

Along with remembering that God was their faithful, welcoming host, God continued to emphasize this feeling of being the stranger, the foreigner, the outsider. Don't forget, he reminded them. *You know exactly what that feels like.*[6]

For centuries to come, this ancient practice of welcoming the stranger became an attractive and distinguishing feature of the church. This receiving of the vulnerable was central to the Christian identity and contributed to the credibility and spread of the gospel.

In the late middle ages however, for a variety of extensive reasons, the notion of hospitality came to be identified with lavish entertaining of the rich and powerful. Hospitality became romanticized, commercialized, and glamorized until it was seen as something that was used to gain favor and power within one's tribe rather than to show favor and give power away. It became a performance rather than a service; lines were drawn, and the audience shifted from those on the margins to those thought to be worthy recipients. Rather than breaking down status distinctions, hospitality became thought of as a practice where they were reinforced.[7] To this day, we struggle—even in our churches—to see through the cultural currents that perpetuate this way of thinking. We now ask, "Who is noticing me?" rather than "Who is unnoticed?"

The notion of hospitality shifted from engagement to entertainment and was emptied almost completely of its true meaning. Matt Chandler describes hospitality as simply "benevolence or good done to those outside someone's normal circle of friends."[8] It invites neighbors to the table who might not believe what you believe, who don't know what you know of the God of the Bible. Why is it such a big deal to God that both Israel and the church today remember to extend hospitality to those outside? Because when we are cold and separate and distant from those around us, we communicate that God is cold and separate and distant.[9] When our posture is warm and gracious and loving, however, we have an opportunity to show that

God is warm and gracious and loving. It's certainly not wrong to open our doors to the people we know and love, but hospitality warrants that we open the door a little wider. Break bread with your people, but save some for those who may not have ever experienced true community or the welcoming touch of God.

Fear of the Stranger

Who are the strangers in our lives? For many of us, they live right around us. They are our neighbors. How many of them remain strangers simply because they are nameless to us? What keeps us from introducing ourselves, asking their names, and stepping into their worlds? Sometimes, if we're honest, we're afraid of them.

A few doors down, our own neighbors are struggling with depression, thoughts of suicide, impossible anxiety, unbearable loneliness, and many have never experienced the richness and incredible blessings that we have in the gospel. But we don't see these vulnerabilities because we feel *we're* the vulnerable ones.

Our posture toward these next-door strangers is characterized by angst and mistrust more than love and welcome. This is not to say that we shouldn't be wise in the process—we should—but we must recognize that the Christian tradition of hospitality is fiercely at odds with the cultural story of isolation or we will continue in these default settings of fear and suspicion.

How powerful it could be in a culture of isolation for you and me to become people who embrace a posture of hospitality by offering and asking for something so simple: our names. Sure, it might be a little scary and potentially awkward at first when we re-introduce ourselves to that neighbor we met years ago but now have forgotten their name and feel too much time has passed. But this is when we go from being unknown to known, from being strangers to friends.

This is what God has done for us, isn't it? He came over, introduced himself, and changed our status from strangers to acquaintances to where Jesus himself ultimately said, "I have called you friends."[10]

From Stranger to Friend

The process of moving from being a stranger to a friend happens when we acquaint ourselves with one another, most importantly when we learn their names. God must've known we needed to see firsthand what it looks like to make the first move. Not only did we need to experience him as our gracious and welcoming host but we also needed to see him take the first step and make the introduction, so to speak. God himself showed us how to move from being a stranger to an acquaintance in one of the most powerful stories of the Bible, when he introduces himself to a man named Moses by telling him his name.[11]

In Exodus 3, when God meets Moses at the burning bush, one of the first things he wants to know is God's name. Moses asks, "[If] the people of Israel . . . ask me, 'What is his name?' what shall I say to them?'"[12]

Unfortunately, our English Bibles don't properly capture God's response. We read, "Say this to the people of Israel, 'I AM has sent me to you.' God also said to Moses, 'Say . . . 'The LORD . . . has sent me to you.'"[13] And when we read the word LORD, we hear a title. But really, the word LORD is a translation of the Hebrew word Yahweh, a name. In all actuality, he says, "Say this to the people of Israel: 'Yahweh[14] has sent me.'"

There is a big difference between a title and a name. A title keeps some distance and formality in the relationship. A title could even define the relationship as one of working value or one of mutual gain. A name, on the other hand, opens the door and makes a space for friendship and relational connection. God, in a sense, says, "Hi, I'm Yahweh," and they move from being strangers to acquaintances, the first step.

Creating a Space Where Change Can Happen

Henri Nouwen said, "Hospitality is not to change people, but to offer them space where change can take place."[15] Although hospitality is a practice, it is first a posture. Hospitality is not agenda driven; instead, it seeks to create spaces where relationships are built and where the gospel can enter in. Hospitality is an overarching attitude and value that compels us to make the first move, to stop what we are doing, say "Hello," and simply trust God with the results.

One of the wonderfully refreshing things about shifting our view in this way is that we begin to recognize there is no "one size fits all." We are free to be our true selves. When we forget that hospitality is a posture and see it primarily as entertainment, it's easy to strive for certain standards of perfection. We find we can become bound by expectations of an ideal. However, when we see it as engagement we are excited to see how God will use our unique wiring, personality, family dynamics, hobbies, interests, and more to bring glory to himself.

What could it look like for you to show hospitality to your neighbors? Are you an introvert or an extrovert? Do you enjoy music? Sports? Animals? Gardening? Exercise? Do you love to throw a party or just go to one? Are you a foodie? Single? Divorced? Married with or without kids? Whether you like to knit or play pickleball, whether you like to go for long runs outside or hole up indoors with a good book, there is no cookie-cutter way to neighbor, and God wants to use you in unique ways to show your neighbors who he is.

Although this kind of hospitality might not wow your friends and family about what a great host or hostess you are, it may just blow your neighbor's mind that someone took the time to learn their name and bring them in so they could begin to taste and see for themselves that the Lord is good.

Hospitality Is Not Just About Giving

It's also important to think about the dynamics of hospitality. In their book *The Art of Neighboring*, authors Pavlok and Runyon note that the "art of receiving" is incredibly important. It's kind of like the art of being needy when it comes to neighboring. We realized early on that we needed to be careful not to show up in our neighborhood as "the person in power," always being the one to give. Runyon says, "We want to be seen as the capable one with all the resources and answers. But when giving is one-sided, it robs the "needy" one of his dignity, because it makes him dependent . . . When giving is two-sided, everyone feels a sense of worth . . . [Receiving] takes humility, it may feel wrong to impose on someone else, and it requires vulnerability." He goes on to say:

> At the end of the day no one wants to feel like a project. We want to feel that we bring something to the table (literally). But when it comes to neighboring well, one of the biggest temptations is to turn neighbors into projects. We put on our "super neighbor cape" and rush out to serve our neighbors and make a difference on our block. This really isn't a bad thing, but if this is all we ever do, then our relationship will be empty. If we don't allow people to meet any of our needs, we limit what God wants to do in our neighborhood and in our life.[16]

Perhaps this idea is akin to what the prophet Jeremiah had in mind when he told the Israelites,

> Thus says the LORD of hosts, the God of Israel, to all the exiles whom I have sent into exile from Jerusalem to Babylon: Build houses and live in them; plant gardens and eat their produce. Take wives and have sons and daughters; take wives for your sons, and give your daughters in marriage, that they may bear sons and daughters; multiply there, and do not decrease. But seek the welfare of the city where I have sent you into exile, and pray to the LORD on its behalf, for in its welfare you will find your welfare.[17]

Why would God command Israel to seek the welfare of the city? They are to build houses, plant gardens, eat the produce, marry, and bear children. They are instructed to give to and serve their pagan neighbors. In this command, there are echoes of God's promise to bless the nations of the earth through Abraham's offspring.

Also contained in this passage is an attitude of receiving. Seek the welfare of the city and pray for it, "For in its welfare you will find your welfare." God's people weren't meant to be self-sufficient. Though they have been given the incredible privilege of being chosen by God to display his character to the world—albeit in captivity—they were still in need and were commanded to receive from the pagan city around them.

It's hard to receive; it's humbling. When we approach neighboring from the perspective that we are always the givers and never the receivers, we forget that Jesus himself was the neighbor who offered the ultimate welcome, but he also made himself vulnerable enough to be welcomed.

So, tomorrow, stop and awkwardly re-introduce yourself to that neighbor you met two years ago and make yourself vulnerable enough to see your neighbor go from being a stranger, to an acquaintance, to hopefully one day a friend. Know that these strangers have been placed as a mercy of God for you. Seek the welfare of your neighborhood, for in its welfare, you will find welfare.

Discussion Guide

Purpose of the Discussion

To discuss how we can move from being strangers to acquaintances to friends with our neighbors.

Chapter Refresher

Scripture shows us that the heartbeat of hospitality is one of love, expressed through a welcoming presence that receives and makes room for the outsider. God continues to remind his people throughout the Old Testament that because they were once strangers and sojourners in Egypt, they are to welcome the strangers and sojourners in their lives. In the New Testament, Paul encourages us to extend the same welcome that we have received in Christ to others. This welcoming posture creates space where strangers can become acquaintances and acquaintances can become friends.

Discussion Questions

1. **Question:** Describe a time when you were on the outside of a group looking in. What was that experience like? How did it shape you?

2. **Read:** So, what do you think it means to live a life of hospitality? Depending on our upbringing, we could all provide different lists of what the word hospitable means to us. We might think of someone who is a good cook or has a well-decorated home. Maybe we think of someone who can host a great party or is generous or who provides a warm environment where others feel at home. While all

of these are good, they provide an incomplete picture when it comes to understanding the heart behind biblical hospitality. As with our definition of what it means to be a good neighbor, sometimes our view of hospitality has been more shaped by the culture than the Bible. In the wise words of Inigo Montoya: "You keep using that word; I do not think it means what you think it means."

Question: List as many things that come to mind when you think about the word hospitality. Looking at the list, try summarizing your definition of hospitality.

3. **Read:** Whereas we might prefer to think of hospitality as merely the entertaining of our family and friends, the biblical writers clearly wanted us to widen our definition. Quite literally, the biblical concept of hospitality is simply to welcome and love the stranger. It says, "Don't forget how you yourself were on the outside. Remember how you were excluded from the Covenant, how you used to not belong? Now that you're in, now that you're near, don't forget about those who still aren't at the table. Remember those who are missing."

Paul says it this way: "Remember that at that time you were separate from Christ, excluded from citizenship in Israel and foreigners to the covenants of the promise, without hope and without God in the world. But now in Christ Jesus you who once were far away have been brought near by the blood of Christ" (Eph. 2:12–13).

Question: As you think about the biblical definition of hospitality, what do you like or dislike about it? Are you more drawn to a cultural definition of hospitality or a biblical definition? Explain why.

4. **Read:** It's hard to think about Christian hospitality without thinking of this welcome from God himself. We begin to see God as our gracious and generous host and see ourselves as his guests. We remember that though we were once strangers, he sought us, welcomed us to himself, hosted us in the wilderness, and provided for all our needs. We hear ourselves saying with the Psalmist, "You prepare a table for me" (Psa. 23:5).

Question: It may be a paradigm shift for some of us to see God as our generous host and ourselves as his guests. How does this mindset inform and empower our hospitality toward our neighbors?

5. **Read:** The process of moving from being a stranger to a friend happens when we acquaint ourselves with one another, most importantly when we learn their names. God must've known we needed to see firsthand what it looks like to make the first move. Not only did we need to experience him as our gracious and welcoming host but we also needed to see him take the first step and make the introduction, so to speak. God himself showed us how to move from being a stranger to an acquaintance in one of the most powerful stories of the Bible, when he

introduces himself to a man named Moses by telling him his name.

Question: When God introduced himself to Moses, he was inviting him and the people of Israel to relate to him in a personal way. Following God's example, introducing ourselves and learning our neighbors' names are two beginning steps toward the practice of hospitality. Who is one neighbor you could introduce yourself to?

6. **Question:** Why is asking for and receiving help from our neighbors so important in the practice of hospitality?

7. **Question:** Henri Nouwnen states, "Hospitality is not to change people, but to offer them space where change can take place."[18] What kind of change would you like to see take place in your neighborhood and in those relationships? Brainstorm different ways you can create spaces where change could happen.

Assignment

As we shift our definition of hospitality from entertainment to engagement and embrace a posture which welcomes the stranger, we recognize this will still play out in different ways for all of us. God has made each of us with different strengths, wiring, interests, and hobbies, and we realize that we can use these gifts and passions to uniquely demonstrate his welcome. Pick one way that you could uniquely show hospitality to your neighbors this week.

Neighboring Prayer for the Week

Lord, you are our great Host who took the first step. You welcomed me in when I was a stranger and you gave me a seat at your table. Help me take that first step toward welcoming my neighbors, especially those who don't yet know you.

PART III

THE PRACTICE OF NEIGHBORING

[DO]

SACRED GROUND: TILLING THE SOIL OF YOUR NEIGHBORHOOD

The Glamour of Go

What one *big* thing will you do for God in your lifetime?!" Passion rang in the speaker's voice, but rather than feeling inspired, my heart sank and I felt deflated. It seemed important here to define the word big. Who would, after all, want to do a *small* thing for God? Whether we work at a law firm, a factory, a church, a fortune 500 company, or are a parent at home buried in laundry and diapers, we yearn to be reminded that all of the exhausting, unseen endeavors of our days are valuable to God and that he sees us. Another woman once said, "I don't want to just bake cookies for God; I want to be on mission." Again, who would want to lower themselves to tasks so mundane and menial as baking? We want to do big things for God, important things. Things that count.

Meanwhile, it may puzzle us that Jesus of Nazareth would stoop to whittle a piece of wood or get sawdust in his beard. If we're honest, Christ's ministry bucket list may even seem a little lackluster compared to ours. If we think the real work is "somewhere out there," we will glaze over the passages where

Jesus waits on the beach with some bread and a charcoal fire so that he can cook breakfast for his disciples. We might not see a fish fry as critical to the mission, but Jesus did. He was a real person in a local community, and he wasn't restless for something grander. When we create a certain sacred-secular split in our minds of what is and isn't valuable work in the kingdom of God, we disconnect from the hard work God has right in front of us. This type of work involves speaking well of our co-workers, gently wiping little hands, and loving those next door.[1]

An Ordinary Mission

Thankfully, Jesus doesn't shy away from the obscure and the commonplace. In fact, he compares his mission to something as ordinary as dirt. Given that agriculture was a big part of their economy, Jesus and the apostles often used soil and farming as a metaphor as they talked about what it meant for the kingdom of God to advance. When Jesus talked about matters of the heart and spiritual realities, he spoke in terms of weeds, good soil, bad soil, and seeds that either scattered or took root. Similarly, Paul likened the spiritual growth that takes place in someone's life to a seed being planted, watered, and grown:

> What then is Apollos? What is Paul? Servants through whom you believed, as the Lord assigned to each. I planted, Apollos watered, but God gave the growth. So neither he who plants nor he who waters is anything, but only God who gives the growth. He who plants and he who waters are one, and each will receive his wages according to his labor. For we are God's fellow workers. You are God's field, God's building.[2]

Unless we're farmers or gardeners, it can be difficult for our modern ears to have a full appreciation for what Jesus and Paul were implying about the growth process. Most of us grab our food from the local grocery store, taking for granted all the TLC that went into producing that carrot. Someone somewhere tilled some soil, sowed some seed, watered it, weeded it, fertilized it, and watched out for pests before eventually harvesting. We all love the harvest, but few of us want to do the hard work of farming. So it is with spiritual work. We love to see a spiritual harvest, where people place their faith in Christ and lives are changed, but sometimes we forget how essential each step is in cultivating the soil to prepare such a harvest.

Harvest Mindset vs. Sowing Mindset

What does it look like to sow spiritually in your neighborhood? Tim Downs defines sowing as the "slow, gradual, behind-the-scenes work that prepares a listener—or a culture—to be able to hear the gospel."[3] When you think about the culture of your neighborhood, imagine it as a sort of field. What is the soil like? Is it soft? Hard? Are there weeds or outside factors that have prevented the seed of the gospel from being established? Even the driest of soils could potentially be made fruitful by God's touch if we were to embrace that sowing is a process and that each step in the process is valuable to God.

Odds are, your neighborhood soil might need some tilling. And if you come in with solely a "harvest mindset," completely focused on end results, you will likely become discouraged and potentially even burn some bridges along the way. A "sowing mindset," however, leads us to dream about what could be while also giving value to each step along the way. The farmer with the "harvest mindset" will eventually stop sowing because he won't have the grit and patience to see the process through to completion. The farmer with the "sowing mindset" plants the seed with the hope that it will one day grow, and it is precisely this hope that helps sustain him through the long process of farming.

In their book *To Transform a City*, Erik Swanson and Sam Williams discuss the difference between having ultimate and ulterior motives.[4] When we have ultimate motives in relationships with our neighbors, we ultimately desire for them to come into a relationship with God through Jesus. Rather than living as undercover Christians, we live out our faith and serve and love our neighbors while building meaningful relationships with them. We enjoy their friendship and we hope, pray, and look for appropriate opportunities to talk about our faith and what God has done in our lives. But it's broader than that, too. We genuinely care about their health, their family—the whole thing. When we have ulterior motives, any act of friendship, love, or service is done exclusively for the single goal of talking about God or getting in a church invite. There's a sneakiness to our neighboring, a bait and switch. When someone says, "I don't want to feel like a project," it's probably because they've interacted with someone who has been operating out of ulterior motives. Read through the following chart on Ulterior and Ultimate Motives.

Ulterior Motives	**Ultimate Motives**
Sees people as projects	Sees people as in process
Elevates the importance of the harvest to the highest level	Views every step in the growth process—tilling, planting, watering, weeding, fertilizing, and harvest—as important and valuable
Limited view of what "counts" as valuable to God	Every step and action along the way "counts"
Compelled to take risks in conversations because spiritual things need to be discussed immediately	Takes appropriate risks in conversations that match the spiritual pace of their neighbor
Narrow view of what it means to love and reach out to a neighbor	Wide view of what it means to love and reach out to a neighbor
Minimizes the importance of the "small stuff" (e.g., just a wave, smile, or short conversation)	Removes "just" from their vocabulary and embraces the importance of each interaction
Goal-oriented in conversations	Enjoys the conversation wherever it goes
Focuses on having the right answers	Focuses on having the right questions
Impatient and easily discouraged; wants immediate change and growth	Long-suffering; knows that growth and change can be gradual

When we live out of ultimate motives rather than ulterior motives, we are freed to dream, serve, be ourselves, and celebrate the little things. When we understand that sowing is a process, we see how every step is essential in the big story of what God is doing. And when we understand that each step is valuable to God, we come to believe that staying is just as important as going. The real work—the *important* work—isn't always what you think. It's sometimes hidden in a pie, an Easter egg, an apartment stairwell, or in a passing conversation at your mailbox. It's a friendly wave that leads to a name that leads to a late night chat on your driveway about divorce or unemployment. As John Stott states, "We love. We go. We serve. And in this we have (or should have) no ulterior motive . . . Love has no need to justify itself. It merely expresses itself in service wherever it sees need."[5] You are freed to love your neighbor with ultimate motives.

The Smallest of Seeds: Removing the Word "Just" from Your Vocabulary

When we sow, we sow with certain expectations. We expect to weed, till, and fertilize the soil. We expect to water the plant again and again. We expect it to take a long time to bear fruit, but we hope that one day it will grow into something so grand that others will be blessed by its shade. We know that no task is unimportant, and we see purpose in each small step because we have a long-term vision for what is to come. Alternatively, we know that if we do not commit to these tasks, we cannot expect growth.

When it comes to seeing God's kingdom flourish in our neighborhoods, why then do we minimize and belittle our efforts by categorizing certain acts as "spiritual" (such as an invitation to church) and others as "unspiritual" (such as a neighborhood block party)? Do we expect God's kingdom to miraculously appear without the sweat and effort required by sowing, weeding, and watering? We must sow with purpose, patience, and great expectancy, knowing that God is at work through seemingly small actions.

Over the years, we've noticed that one of the biggest hindrances to embracing ultimate motives and a sowing mindset can be found in the four-letter word *just*. We say, "I've just prayed." "It's just a wave." "It's just dinner." When we use this kind of language, we minimize God's work. And what we're really saying is "What difference could any of this make anyway?"

Jesus reminded us that small seeds make a big difference. Perhaps he was taking shade under an overgrown tree or shrub when he shared one of the most powerful analogies in Scripture, recorded in Mark chapter 4:

> And he said, "With what can we compare the kingdom of God, or what parable shall we use for it? It is like a grain of mustard seed, which, when sown on the ground, is the smallest of all the seeds on earth, yet when it is sown it grows up and becomes larger than all the garden plants and puts out large branches, so that the birds of the air can make nests in its shade."[6]

Did you catch it? Jesus took an interest in "the smallest of seeds." Of course we know he's speaking in hyperbole and that the mustard seed wasn't *truly* the smallest seed, but when you're holding a mustard seed in your hands, it sure feels pretty small. Maybe that's part of his point. When we're neighboring in God's story, many of our actions feel so small and so mundane that they might as well be the smallest of seeds we could plant for God's kingdom. Yet we forget that this is precisely the means of grace used by God to produce the large, fruit-bearing, shade-making, nest-providing growth that we see years after it's been sown.

There are no insignificant tasks. It's never "just" a prayer, "just" a wave, "just" an Easter egg hunt, or "just" learning a neighbor's name. Removing the word "just" from our neighboring vocabulary is imperative if we are going to engage in the low and slow process of seeing the kingdom of God shoot up in our neighborhoods and flourish in our neighbors' lives.

Start to see yourself in God's big story of redemption. It's a story where each step of the process has value and where God wants to use you—your personality, your gifts, and even your limits—in unique ways.

Where to Begin in Breaking Up the Ground

1. Initiate.

Taking initiative is one of the simplest, most powerful things you can do as a neighbor. It doesn't have to be anything mind-blowing. Consider these suggestions:

- Pray for your neighbors, for your neighborhood, and for yourself as you neighbor.
- Wave to neighbors as you walk and drive through your neighborhood.
- Say "Hello" to your neighbors as you're walking, driving, or in your yard.
- Print (from Google Maps) or draw a map of your neighborhood, then write names on the map of who lives where.

- Introduce yourself to neighbors and learn their names. Jot down names and facts in a note on your phone to help you remember them.

- Reintroduce yourself to a neighbor whose name you've forgotten or to someone you've lived by for a while. It might feel awkward or "too late" to ask, but it's a powerful step to take and worth it to reestablish a relationship with them.

- If you have neighbors who are from a different country or who have names that are difficult for you to pronounce, ask them to help you say their names correctly and then use their names the next time you see them.

- If you see a neighbor outside when you get home, instead of pulling into your driveway and going straight inside and closing the door, try coming out, saying "Hi," and asking a question that could lead to a short touchpoint.

- If you see someone moving into your neighborhood, drop off a simple welcome basket. (Google "Housewarming Basket" for easy ideas.)

- Engage on your neighborhood's social media pages or create one.

2. Serve.

Do something to better your neighborhood. Ask yourself, "If I were to move, would I have left my neighborhood better than I found it?" Why is this important? Because whatever our context—whether we live downtown or out-of-town, whether we're urbanites or suburbanites—our neighborhoods have real needs. Serving is one of the most important things we can do as neighbors; when we serve we push back against the effects of sin's wintery curse, both externally (bringing repair where there has been disrepair) and internally (bringing connection where there has been isolation). This is where snow melts, where hearts are thawed, and where death is turned to life in spring. Try one or two of these suggestions as a way to serve your neighbors:

- Look for ways to serve the vulnerable in your apartment building or neighborhood.
- Volunteer to serve on the Homeowner's Association.
- Create a tool-sharing list (snow and leaf blowers, extension ladders, carpet cleaners, etc.)
- Host a book exchange or toy swap.
- Participate in neighborhood trail repair.
- Share fresh produce with other neighbors.
- Pick up trash as you walk.
- Bake cookies for neighbors.
- Ask a few neighbors about scheduling a yard work day and then help each other.
- Partner with a "clean up your city" event or plan an Arbor Day party.
- Coordinate a food, coat, or backpack drive (or partner with a school or church to do so).
- Organize a neighborhood community garden or tree planting.
- Start or participate in a Neighborhood Watch Program.

- Offer to organize meals for neighbors in need (for those who've had surgery, lost a loved one, had a baby, etc.).
- Shovel snow for a neighbor.

3. Cultivate.

When we first began this journey, I (Elizabeth) wanted to get to know our neighbors, but I felt like we needed an excuse to do so. That first fish fry was our chance to begin building some relationships. From there, we posted on our neighborhood Facebook page that we were going to host an Easter egg hunt. I think there were only six or seven kids there (and we have four of our own so what does that tell you about humble beginnings?), yet this is where we met Nathan and Cathy, who would become some of our dearest neighbors. I remember Cathy saying to me that day, "Well hey, if you ever want to do some more neighboring things I'd love to help." I looked at her blankly and asked, "Like what?" She suggested a block party and from there we became a dynamic duo. It would've been easy at the time to consider our little Easter egg hunt insignificant but looking back it was one of the most important things we've ever done. It wasn't "just" an Easter egg hunt. Rather, it was the first step in the development of a vibrant community. More importantly, it was our first glimpse of God's curse-cancelling power at work in the lives of so many of our neighbors.

What could you try? What little barbeque or porch party could give you an excuse to meet your neighbors? What's something that fits your season of life and your neighboring context? Here are a few ideas for you to try or translate to your neighborhood:

- Host a dinner or dessert. Keep it simple and ask/allow people to bring something. This helps everyone feel a sense of ownership and participation in the get-together.
- Walk with a neighbor or set up a walking group that meets at specific times during the week. Invite other neighbors to join.
- Host a monthly coffee and donuts gathering outside your house thirty minutes before people leave to take kids to school.
- Organize or participate in a walking school bus.
- Ask for help with physical needs (borrowing yard, home, or kitchen tools, landscaping, moving furniture, needing sugar or eggs, etc.).
- Ask for neighbors' expertise (for example, if your neighbor is good at gardening, ask for advice or help. If a neighbor is good at making pies, ask if they'd be willing to come over and teach you, etc.).
- Ask for recommendations (local plumber, electrician, mechanic, etc.).
- Suggest a "dog playdate."
- Get an inexpensive, portable fire pit and invite some neighbors to hang out and make s'mores.
- Host a game night, watch or go to a movie together, or set up an outdoor movie.
- Plan an Easter egg hunt.
- Help neighborhood kids create a lemonade stand.
- Organize a neighborhood block party.
- Participate in a yard sale. Co-host it with neighbors on either side of you.

- Host a spaghetti night or a pancake breakfast.
- Organize a neighborhood book discussion.
- Coordinate a progressive dinner with a few neighbors.

A Note on Conflict

Neighboring is messy and conflict is a normal part of relationships. We know intuitively that it's to be expected with our neighbors, but the truth is it can be really deflating and cause us to lose sight of the bigger picture. As believers, we still struggle with sins of entitlement, tribalism, and short-sightedness. So, before we jump to overly grim conclusions about our neighbors, we need to remember that we all need a Savior. In fact, we aren't surprised when we've unintentionally offended someone or when neighbors across the way aren't on speaking terms. We remind ourselves that there is a normal wear and tear to living beside one another and we're not going to let things end before they've even begun. A few tips for this difficult practice:

- Acceptance is not agreement. People and ideas are separate. This means you can accept the person even if you don't agree with their ideas.
- Don't let small things become big things.
- When a conversation is necessary, communicate your concern directly with the neighbor involved. Don't gossip or spread rumors. Keep your explanation brief and your words gracious, paving the way for peaceful resolution.

- Forgive as Christ has forgiven you. Then forgive again. And again.

If the soil of your neighborhood has become dry
and hardened, don't despair. Perhaps with some watering and tilling through ordinary relationships, de-
layed gratification, and staying precisely where you
are, you could start to see glimpses of the kingdom of
God breaking into the most unexpected places.

Discussion Guide

Purpose of the Discussion

Compare and contrast a sowing mindset versus a harvest mindset.

Chapter Refresher

We all love the harvest, but few of us want to do the hard work of farming. So it is with spiritual work. We love to see a spiritual harvest, where people place their faith in Christ and lives are changed, but sometimes we forget how essential each step is in cultivating the soil to prepare such a harvest. As we remove the word "just" from neighboring vocabulary and think with ultimate motives rather than ulterior motives, we are freed to value and enjoy the low and slow of neighboring.

Discussion Questions

1. **Read:** It may puzzle us that Jesus of Nazareth would stoop to whittle a piece of wood or get sawdust in his beard. If we're honest, Christ's ministry bucket list may even seem a little lackluster compared to ours. If we think the real work is "somewhere out there," we will glaze over the passages where Jesus waits on the beach with some bread and a charcoal fire so that he can cook breakfast for his disciples. We might not see a fish fry as critical to the mission, but Jesus did. He was a real person in a local community, and he wasn't restless for something grander. When we create a certain sacred-secular split in our minds of what is and isn't

valuable work in the kingdom of God, we disconnect from the hard work God has right in front of us.

Question: Spend a few minutes listing "glamorous" things you might like to do for God. Then list "ordinary" things that you are called to do.

2. **Watch:** To help gain a better understanding of the growth process, search for the short video on YouTube called "Growing and Using Wheat at Home." Go to settings and set the video to double speed. Watch the first six minutes.

    Discuss: List everything that stands out to you about the process of growing wheat and share those as a group.

3. **Discuss:** As you think about your neighborhood context, try to describe the spiritual condition of the soil. What experiences or interactions lead you to these conclusions?

4. **Read:** When we have ultimate motives in relationships with our neighbors, we ultimately desire for them to come into a relationship with God through Jesus. Rather than living as undercover Christians, we live out our faith and serve and love our neighbors while building meaningful relationships with them. We enjoy their friendship and we hope, pray, and look for appropriate opportunities to talk about our faith and what God has done in our lives. But it's broader than that, too. We genuinely care about their health, their family—the whole thing. When

we have ulterior motives, any act of friendship, love or service is done exclusively for the single goal of talking about God or getting in a church invite. There's a sneakiness to our neighboring, a bait and switch. When someone says, "I don't want to feel like a project," it's probably because they've interacted with someone who has been operating out of ulterior motives.

Question: Have you ever been on the receiving end of someone with ulterior motives? What do you think it looks like to have ultimate rather than ulterior motives with your neighbors?

5. **Read:** "With what can we compare the kingdom of God, or what parable shall we use for it? It is like a grain of mustard seed, which, when sown on the ground, is the smallest of all the seeds on earth, yet when it is sown it grows up and becomes larger than all the garden plants and puts out large branches, so that the birds of the air can make nests in its shade" (Mark 4:30–32).

Did you catch it? Jesus took an interest in "the smallest of seeds." Of course we know he's speaking in hyperbole and that the mustard seed wasn't *truly* the smallest seed, but when you're holding a mustard seed in your hands, it sure feels pretty small. Maybe that's part of his point. When we're neighboring in God's story, many of our actions feel so small and so mundane that they might as well be the smallest of seeds we could plant for God's kingdom. Yet we forget that this is precisely the means of grace used by God to produce the large, fruit-bearing, shade-making, nest-providing growth that we see years after it's been sown.

Question: How does the parable of the mustard seed encourage you to dream about what God could do in your neighborhood?

6. **Read:** There are no insignificant tasks. It's never "just" a prayer, "just" a wave, "just" an Easter egg hunt, or "just" learning a neighbor's name. Removing the word "just" from our neighboring vocabulary is imperative if we are going to engage in the low and slow process of seeing the kingdom of God shoot up in our neighborhoods and flourish in our neighbors' lives. Start to see yourself in God's big story of redemption. It's a story where each step of the process has value, and where God wants to use you—your personality, your gifts, and even your limits—in unique ways.

Question: Why do you think we tend to minimize our neighboring efforts by prefacing them with the word "just"? What else needs to shift in your thinking for you to embrace a sowing mindset in neighboring?

Assignment

Take thirty seconds of silence and ask God to show you one simple next step you could take to till the soil in your neighborhood. Write it down and share it with the group.

Neighboring Prayer for the Week

Lord, I desire for my neighborhood to be a place where the gospel can take root and flourish. Help me value the process of tilling and cultivating the soil of my neighborhood. May your kingdom come in my neighborhood.

GOSPEL-MOTIVATED CONVERSATIONS

Read Luke 18:18–30

I f this passage sounds familiar, it might be because this is the second time we've seen someone come to Jesus and ask the question "What must I do to inherit eternal life?" Can you imagine a neighbor of yours coming to you and asking what they needed to do to inherit eternal life? In both cases, Jesus is thrown a softball. In both instances, he indirectly answers the question. Did he whiff? What happened?

The first time this happened, we read of the expert in the law eight chapters prior who asked this to test Jesus. It's a little easier to imagine why Jesus might not have responded clearly in Luke 10 considering the lawyer's lousy motives, but here this young ruler seems genuinely curious. Why not answer him as plainly as possible? What can we learn from the way Jesus navigates conversation with this rich young neighbor that could help us as we seek to have meaningful conversations with our neighbors?

Neighbors None and Done

If we're honest, many of us feel nervous about the mere thought of asking our neighbor's names, let alone sharing our faith with them. Though there can be something really exciting about entering into these conversations, it's a ginormous step outside our comfort zone. Reading current religious trends and online headlines hardly provides much inspiration. It doesn't surprise us to read that in the last fifteen years, America has seen its sharpest decline in church attendance and biblical literacy to date.[1] Fewer Americans identify as Christians, associating Christianity with words like intolerance, judgmentalism, and hypocrisy. Meanwhile, the number of religiously unaffiliated adults has dramatically increased. The 56 million religiously unaffiliated adults in the U.S. have sometimes been called the "Nones" (as in "None of the above") or the "Dones" (as in "Done with religion").[2]

Tim Keller highlights how these cultural shifts have affected gospel-centered conversations over time. The gospel has not changed, but conversations about the gospel have. Keller writes,

> People simply do not have the necessary background knowledge to hear a gospel address and immediately understand who God is, what sin is, who Jesus is, and what repentance and faith are in a way that enables them to make an intelligent commitment. They often have far too many objections and beliefs for the gospel to be readily plausible to them. Therefore, most people in the West need to be welcomed into a community long enough for them to hear multiple expressions of the gospel—both formal and informal—from individuals and teachers. As this happens in community, non-believers come to understand the character of God, sin, and grace. Many of their objections are answered through this

process. Because they are "on the inside" and involved in ongoing relationships with Christians, they can imagine themselves as Christians and see how the faith fleshes out in real life.[3]

Consequently, we no longer have certain luxuries in conversations about belief that we had twenty and thirty years ago. Our previous methods for communicating the gospel were innovative for their time but assumed so much of the listener that just isn't true anymore. Our post-Christian neighbors aren't sure there is any kind of afterlife, do not believe the Bible to be the inspired Word of God, don't hold that there are any moral, transcultural absolutes, and think that we may in fact suffer from a God delusion. The church is having to rethink and redefine what a "spiritual conversation" even is. Maybe that's a good thing.

Does it count as spiritual only if you say Jesus's name, mention church, or give a whole gospel presentation? Or do we need to back up further? Could a spiritual conversation include topics ranging as broadly as self-image, depression, race, career, and even gardening? What if those are some of the most significant, ground-breaking, seed-watering, soil-fertilizing, spiritual conversations you have? Remember Paul's words: "I planted, Apollos watered, but God gave the growth. So neither he who plants nor he who waters is anything, but only God who gives the growth."[4]

We know that the good news of the gospel needs to be spoken and heralded.

"Consequently, faith comes from hearing the message, and the message is heard through the word about Christ."[5] But if we don't pause to evaluate our approach, broaden our view of what is valuable and what counts, and embrace the wisdom of nuance, the church will inevitably experience a degree of Evangelism Insanity; we'll keep doing the same things over and over while expecting different results, or we'll keep avoiding the conversation altogether.

It sounds daunting to engage an ever-changing culture with a never-changing gospel. But what if you knew there were some very practical things you could do in conversations that could turn the head of your "none" and "done" neighbor, leading them to reevaluate the claims of Jesus?

Here's something that might encourage you. Eight-two percent of non-religious people said they would be willing to have a conversation with a Christian about their faith if the Christian could do these five things (*though they didn't believe Christians could*):[6]

1. Be present and listen (Follow the conversation).
2. Walk in their shoes (Understand their story).
3. Find common ground (Build a relational bridge).
4. Talk like a real person (Don't use words they can't understand).
5. Create a better story (How does God relate to my life now?).

Did you catch that? They would be willing to have a spiritual conversation if the believer could do these five things . . . but never mind, because they couldn't. But *what if,* as believers, we could and we did? Let that sink in a little. What if your next-door "nones" and "dones" are not as done as they let on? You have the opportunity through the work of God's Spirit to ask good questions, use some indirect communication, and potentially bring life-changing clarity to the gospel.

Be Present and Listen

When this rich young ruler came to Jesus to talk about "spiritual things," Jesus was listening carefully. He wasn't scrolling through his phone or waiting for him to finish his sentences so that he could run through his typical script. Being present allowed him to thoughtfully choose a question ("Why do you call me good?") that would begin to chip away at this guy's distorted view of goodness, and in doing so, begin to help him see his need for grace and lead him toward the next step.

In Mark's account of this story, he says, "And Jesus, looking at him, loved him . . ."[7] We see Jesus demonstrating this love as he is present, listening, and asking questions. David Augsburger wisely writes, "Being heard is so close to being loved that for the average person, they are almost indistinguishable."[8] If you've ever had someone slow down, ask you some good questions, and really listen to you, then you know how true this is. Jonathan Chatraw adds, "Of course we need to speak and make appeals for the gospel, but listening and hearing people out—in a culture where people feel like they have to get their points out before they get cut off—can plow the ground for gospel conversation."[9]

Practicing Gospel-Motivated Listening

- Make space in your lives for interactions with your neighbors by going for regular walks outside, stopping to say "Hello," and initiating a conversation by asking questions.

- Actively engage in the practice of turning your thoughts from the concerns and details of your own life to the concerns and details of your neighbor's life.

- Ask questions about your neighbor's beliefs and experiences with faith and church and simply listen appreciatively and sympathetically.

- Practice empathy and walking in their shoes by saying, "I can understand how you'd feel that way."

- Refrain from expressing counterpoints and playing devil's advocate.

- Open the door for deeper conversation by asking a follow-up question or saying, "I'd love to hear more about that."

- Find and talk about areas of common ground with your neighbor (e.g., a shared stage of life, a shared hobby, mutual concern, common interest in business, the arts, etc.).

- Make a short note on your phone so you can remember names or other important details.

Learning Indirect Communication from Jesus

What else can we learn from Jesus as we attempt to have meaningful conversations with our neighbors? If you've ever felt like you weren't doing enough by "just listening" and asking questions in spiritual conversations, then this next principle might also seem like small potatoes. Quite the contrary, learning indirect communication from Jesus is one of the most effective skills we can develop in gospel-motivated conversations.

If you've ever taken a communication class, you may have heard of the 7% rule which states that only seven percent of our communication is verbal. The vast majority of what we say to our neighbors is through non-verbal cues. But what about our verbal communication? Have you ever considered the difference between direct and indirect communication? When we speak directly, the meaning is explicit. It's clear, obvious, and "to the point." But sometimes we choose to speak with more subtlety where the meaning is implied or has to be uncovered.

It's probably an understatement to say that Jesus had a leg up on us in navigating these types of conversations. He knew when to be explicit and when to be implicit, when to press in and when to let up. And yet, when we see the way Jesus handles the rich young ruler, we could question his choices. It seems he prefers an oddly indirect form of communication.

Jesus thoughtfully and intentionally steers the conversation by reminding him of God's holy standards. "You know the commandments: 'Do not commit adultery, Do not murder, Do not steal, Do not bear false witness, Honor your father and mother.'" This wealthy leader can barely get two sentences in without revealing that his theology is a little dicey. Instead of responding in humility, his over-inflated self joins the chorus of every other human as he proclaims, "All these I have kept from my youth."

Does Jesus correct him? Does he say, "Listen, hot shot, let me help you with your lack of self-awareness. You honestly think you've been perfect your whole life? God alone is perfect; and your arrogance makes you all the more in need of a Savior"? No, Jesus is drawing out the conversation.

Whereas we might shoot it to him straight, Jesus seemed to know something we don't. He knew, in the words of Jerram Barrs, that "showing the beauty of righteousness or the ugliness of sin is a far more effective way of bringing people to conviction than simply telling them that they are sinners."[10] He prefers the wisdom of indirection. Luke tells us, "When Jesus heard this, he said to him, 'You still lack one thing. Sell everything you have and give to the poor, and you will have treasure in heaven. Then come, follow me.' When he heard this, he became very sad, because he was very wealthy."

So, let's recap: Rich guy comes to Jesus and asks, "What do I do to inherit eternal life?" Jesus says that only perfect people can get into heaven (i.e., no one). Now rich guy is feeling really good, because he's got this! He's practically perfect in every way. But then Jesus pulls back the curtain and exposes that this guy's god is actually his money. He wants him to see the ugliness of his greed; this is not only what will keep him from God but it's also the very thing that will show him his need for a Savior.

What comes next is supposed to be the moment when the ruler says, "Oh, I get it. Jesus, money is the love of my life that drives all of my other loves. And there is a greed flowing through my veins that has poisoned me. I realize now that I have *not* kept the commandments from my youth, not a single one of them. Unless you give me new life, I will never change." Ideally, yes. But it didn't go that way. Jesus is asking questions and making statements to poke holes in his worldview. And just as he had the wisdom to make room in the conversation for subtlety and self-discovery, he also had the patience to let him walk away sad. He's guiding the conversation, but he's not forcing it.

Eugene Peterson said, "Jesus was the master of indirection. The parables are subversive. His hyperboles are indirect. There is a kind of outrageous quality to them that defies common sense, but later on the understanding comes."[11] When asked if evangelicals are being too direct with the gospel, Peterson replied,

> I'd hesitate to say we're too frontal because that's part of proclamation: the Kingdom of God is here, repent, believe the gospel. But, yes, we need to do a lot more indirection. That's basically what a poet or a novelist does. I wouldn't say we need to do less frontal work with the gospel, we just need to do more of the subversive stuff.[12]

In our post-Christian culture, practicing the art of indirection is a necessary skill for breaking the ground in our neighborhoods.

C.S. Lewis, one of the most effective apologists of all times, also embraced indirect communication as a powerful means of revealing truth and undermining doubt. Lewis said, "What we want is not more little books about Christianity, but more little books by Christians on other subjects—with their Christianity latent."[13] Let's put this in neighboring terms. Consider that what our non-believing neighbors may need most from us initially is not little conversations about Christianity—though they need those too—but rather little conversations by Christians on other subjects with our Christianity latent. Or to say it another way, your neighbors need to hear you talk about education, the arts, science, technology, politics, and economics with your Christian worldview interwoven into the fabric of the conversation.

The following chart will help us compare and contrast the differences in these communication styles. Though one is not better than the other, there is wisdom in knowing when to use each one.

Direct Communication	Indirect Communication
Explicit (clear, obvious)	Implicit (implied)
To the point	Subtle
Meaning given	Meaning sought

Do not equate the use of indirect communication with having ulterior motives. One can have the ultimate motive of seeing their neighbor know Jesus and use either communication style. With indirect communication, we're not playing the game of bait and switch; we are simply not saying it all on the first date. It works best when we confidently self-identify with Christ and live out the gospel, albeit in a broken way, but do so with a sensitivity to timing, wisdom, and nuance.

So, just as there are times to speak directly, there are also times when we are called to engage in conversations where the gospel sleeps quietly in how you handle your anxiety, experience grief, talk about the ups and downs of the stock market, or walk through seasons of singleness, infertility, and parenting. Don't be troubled when all is not said and seeds lie dormant and underdeveloped. In that dissonance, pray! Pray knowing that God is at work and that "the Kingdom of God is like a mustard seed."

Practicing Indirect Communication

- Self-identify as a Christian (e.g., through conversation, mentions of going to church, thoughtful social media posts, etc.).
- Engage in pressing cultural conversations and speak from an informed perspective.
- Pick up a book written from a Christian worldview that could help your indirect communication as it relates to work, the arts, racial relations, etc. Here are a few suggestions: *Work Matters* by Tom Nelson, *Echoes of Eden: Reflections on Christianity, Literature, and the Arts* by Jerram Barrs, and *Disunity in Christ: Uncovering the Hidden Forces that Keep Us Apart* by Christena Cleveland.
- Introduce your neighbors to other believers and plan an activity where they can experience an informal taste of Christian community without it being a "Christian event."
- Listen to a neighbor share about a challenge they're experiencing and mention that you will pray regularly for them.
- Encourage where you see God's image in your neighbor.

Gospel Clarity

Just as it's important to indirectly flavor our conversations, it's also important that we are able to be direct and communicate with gospel clarity. What does that look like practically to determine appropriate next steps and talking points? Here are a few principles to help us navigate how and when to be direct in conversations.

First, we need to self-identify as Christians. Though it might sound like one of the simplest steps, it can honestly be terrifying. Peter himself was too scared to do this at one time, and when asked if he was with Christ, he recoiled with a "Who, me?!" Identifying as a Christ-follower is one of the best things you can do to bring sincerity and genuineness to your conversations. When you post a picture of your small group or share casually about going to church over the weekend or about God meeting you in a current struggle, you are opening up the conversation. Then as your friendships grow, your neighbors are connecting with the real you, the one who follows Jesus not from a distance but up close. When the time comes that they are ready and need a Christian friend, you are right there next door.

Second, we need to ask the question "At what spiritual pace is my neighbor running?" We must consider their pace and ask, "Am I keeping in step with them, or am I outpacing them? Do I need to slow down, listen sympathetically, and engage in more indirect spiritual conversations? Are they beginning to pick up speed, needing a more direct challenge and encouragement to take the next step toward Jesus?"

Third, we need to remember to take risks in conversations. When you're listening sympathetically, using the wisdom of restraint in indirect communication, and maintaining awareness of the pace the other person is running, you may need to remind yourself that it's good to take risks in conversation when it comes to sharing your faith. It's vulnerable to share what God is doing in your life. It's scary to invite your neighbor to a book discussion or to church, to give someone a Bible, or to challenge how God might be at work in them. We risk being rejected, sidelined, and misunderstood. Maybe worse. But what might feel like an initial rejection could be just a snapshot in that person's life. We don't always have the bigger picture of what God is doing or will do when we put ourselves out there in these conversations.

Practicing Gospel Clarity

- Invite a neighbor to venues where they hear the gospel communicated and discussed, such as an open forum, worship service, etc.
- Offer a book or audio recording about a Christian issue and have them over to discuss.
- Share a current difficulty in your life and how you see God at work. When sharing about something related to your faith experience, whether theology or church activities, avoid using insider language or consider explaining terms that might be unfamiliar to an outsider.
- Share how God has helped—or is helping you—work through intellectual doubts you've had in your relationship with God. What answers have you found that have helped you build a more robust faith?
- Begin a neighborhood Bible study.
- Encourage and challenge your neighbor to consider an aspect of God's character or a promise of God that could be meaningful to them in their current circumstances.
- Share your spiritual narrative, a brief testimony of your Christian experience. Emphasize how Jesus is making a difference in your life now (e.g., your season of life, your job, self-image, relationships with others, etc.).

- Regularly read the Bible together (perhaps the Gospels) with one neighbor to discuss the character of Jesus.

- Share the basics of the Christian faith with your friend. Explain how to become a Christian and invite them to make a commitment.

- Host a book discussion written by a Christian author on a relevant topic such as *The Purpose Driven Life* by Rick Warren, *Afraid of All the Things* by Scarlet Hiltibidal or *The Color of Compromise* by Jemar Tisby.

- Use social media to share resources that are currently helping you grow in your faith (e.g., a recent sermon, liturgical prayer, blog post, podcast, etc.)

Conclusion

The rich young ruler walked away sad that day. We read,

> But when he heard these things, he became very sad, for he was extremely rich. Jesus, seeing that he had become sad, said, "How difficult it is for those who have wealth to enter the kingdom of God! For it is easier for a camel to go through the eye of a needle than for a rich person to enter the kingdom of God." Those who heard it said, "Then who can be saved?" But he said, "What is impossible with man is possible with God."[14]

Was that the end of the story? We don't know for sure, but the early church seems to have identified this young neighbor as Joseph of Arimathea—the rich man who provided the tomb for Jesus's body after his crucifixion. Jerram Barrs says,

If this was indeed the man, then one day we can ask him how long it was before the worldly sorrow he experienced the day he met Jesus was turned to a godly sorrow that led him back to Jesus, and on to repentance and faith. Although it was impossible for the young man to change his heart on his own, nothing is impossible for Jesus.[15]

There are neighbors of yours who have considered Jesus and walked away sad. From their perspective and yours, they are none and done. But you don't have the end of the story. Some of them, in fact, through ordinary conversations with ordinary you—in a place as non-glamourous as their own neighborhood—will reconsider Jesus altogether. And some of them will slowly move from their previous story of comfort, seclusion, and self-sufficiency into God's Big Story of Redemption. They will see, just like you did, that they are placed for a purpose, and they will start to see their neighbors as glorious ruins and prove to be a neighbor. They will welcome the stranger and join God's mission by becoming seed planters and soil tillers. And they will never give up on the neighbor who says they're done with God, because just like Jesus said, "What is impossible with man is possible with God."[16]

Discussion Guide

Purpose of the Discussion

Choose one step you can take to listen well, use indirect communication, or practice gospel clarity in conversations with your neighbors.

Chapter Refresher

If we're honest, many of us feel nervous about the mere thought of asking our neighbors' names, let alone sharing our faith with them. There have also been massive cultural shifts over time that have affected our gospel-centered conversations. The gospel has not changed but conversations about the gospel have. As we shift from a "one size fits all" approach, we can reimagine what it means to engage an ever-changing culture with a never-changing gospel. We can learn from Jesus how to practice gospel-motivated listening, indirect communication, and gospel clarity.

Discussion Questions

1. **Read:** Both the rich young ruler in Luke 18 and the Bible scholar in Luke 10 approach Jesus with the same question: "What must I do to inherit eternal life?" In both instances he indirectly answers the question. Did he whiff? What happened?

    Question: Take a minute to share as a group. Imagine a specific neighbor comes to you with the question "What must I do to inherit eternal life?" What would you be feeling? What would you say? Would you respond as Jesus did?

2. **Read:** Here's something that might encourage you. 82% of non-religious people said they would be willing to have a conversation with a Christian about their faith if the Christian could do these five things (*though they didn't believe Christians could*):

    - Be present and listen (Follow the conversation).

    - Walk in their shoes (Understand their story).

    - Find common ground (Build a relational bridge).

    - Talk like a real person (Don't use words they can't understand).

    - Create a better story (How does God relate to my life now?).[17]

    Question: Does it surprise you to hear that 82% of non-religious people would be open to having a spiritual conversation with a Christian if they could do these five things? Which of these five things are you most excited to incorporate in your interactions with neighbors and why?

3. **Read:** If you've ever had someone slow down, ask you some good questions, and really listen to you, then you know how powerful listening can be. Jonathan Chatraw, in an article entitled *Ask and You Shall Evangelize,*

states, "Of course we need to speak and make appeals for the gospel, but listening and hearing people out—in a culture where people feel like they have to get their points out before they get cut off—can plow the ground for gospel conversation."[18]

Question: If listening is such a powerful gift we can offer in conversations, why do we struggle so much to offer it?

4. **Read:** Does it count as spiritual only if you say Jesus's name, mention church, or give a whole gospel presentation? Or do we need to back up further? Could a spiritual conversation include topics ranging as broadly as self-image, depression, race, career, and even gardening? What if those are some of the most significant, ground-breaking, seed-watering, soil-fertilizing, spiritual conversations you have? Remember Paul's words: "I planted the seed, Apollos watered it, but God has been making it grow.[7] So neither the one who plants nor the one who waters is anything, but only God, who makes things grow" (1 Cor. 3:6–7).

Question: As we think about incorporating indirect communication into conversations with non-believing neighbors, it stretches how we define a "spiritual conversation." What about this excites you? What challenges you?

5. **Read:** Eugene Peterson said, "Jesus was the master of indirection. The parables are subversive. His hyperboles are indirect. There is a kind of outrageous quality to them that

defies common sense, but later on the understanding comes."[19]

Consider that what our non-believing neighbors may need most from us initially is not little conversations about Christianity—though they need those too—but rather little conversations by Christians on other subjects with our Christianity latent. Or to say it another way, your neighbors need to hear you talk about education, the arts, science, technology, politics, and economics with your Christian worldview interwoven into the fabric of the conversation.

Discuss: Choose one of the topics above (or come up with your own) and brainstorm ways in which your Christian worldview could be latent in a conversation with a neighbor.

6. **Discuss:** Share a specific, practical way you can imagine the following in conversations with your neighbors: (1) Self-identifying as a Christian (2) Identifying the spiritual pace of your neighbor and keeping in step with them, and (3) Taking risks in conversations.

7. **Question:** How does reading the story of the rich young ruler give you hope for how God might work in your neighbors' lives?

Assignments

(1) Choose one suggestion from both Practicing Indirect Communication and Practicing Gospel Clarity that would be a good next step for you.

(2) Take thirty seconds of silence and ask God to show you one simple next step that you could take in the area of neighboring. Share that next step with the group.

Neighboring Prayer for the Week

Lord, when I think about talking about my faith with my neighbors sometimes it seems like a daunting task. Please help me listen well, flavor my conversations with the gospel, and take steps of faith to talk about you with my neighbors.

ACKNOWLEDGMENTS

Tasha, you are a sage. Thank you for that first Zoom call so long ago. Though our ideas were muddled and all over the place, you responded with such a gracious enthusiasm that made us believe we should continue. From there, you championed us every step of the way. Thanks to your mentorship, we dove into the world of learning objectives, Bloom's Taxonomy, visual aids, and beta-testing. We owe you a huge debt of gratitude.

Thank you Ginger, Pearl, June, and Annie. You are the best little neighbors anyone could ask for. Even though you don't pick up your bikes or your rollerblades, scooters or helmets, and you leave your socks on other people's driveways, you endear people to you because you love with a big, honest love. Thank you for all those bedtime prayers. Keep letting your light shine for Jesus. You can have all the Cheetos you want at the block party but please wear shoes, if possible.

Thank you to Jeremy, our publisher. One of the biggest surprise gifts throughout all of this has been the sovereignly timed partnership with Gospel-Centered Discipleship. We have been blessed by your heart for discipleship, your humility, and intellectual flexibility. Lauren and Alexandra—wowza. We'd be remiss to not acknowledge your editorial gifts, but you've ruined us. Now we can't write emails or send texts without wishing you'd look over them first. Laura, you nailed the cover. Because of you, our book a face that says, *no matter where you live, this is for you*. Benjamin—thank you for turning our manuscript into a real book and teaching us how to make an em dash—now if we only knew where to put them. Jenn, Cheryl, Byron—and so many other smart people who read our manuscript—your feedback was invaluable. And a ridiculously long-standing ovation for all the people who took our unedited, less-than-stellar first draft and graciously beta-tested it in your small groups and other settings. David and Kelli, Brian and Rachel, Tim and Aubrey, Clayton and Jules, Steve and Amy, Kelly, Josh and Allie, and our own small group—thanks for being the guinea pigs. We wish we could've given you something more refined and finished to use but your help is what got us here.

Thanks to all our ministry partners who have prayed and generously supported us for twenty years. Any small group that is changed, any neighbor who is reached, any life that is touched is the result of God's work through your giving and prayers. Mom and Dad Templeton, thank you for lovingly and faithfully praying this into existence. Mom and Dad McKinney, thank you for serving us so tirelessly, especially through watching the kids so we could work on this. Jane—eternal gratitude for all the time and grace you poured into that awkward freshman. And a huge thanks to The Crossing. What a gift it's been to grow as we teach our content and also be part of the staff team with you all. Thanks Dave and Jeannette for bringing us in.

Last but not least, thank you to our neighbors. Thank you for loving us, helping us keep our kids alive, for all the hand-me downs, and for sharing the vision of a neighborhood community. You've opened your lives, let people walk through your yards, shared countless meals, and helped clean up after all the block parties. You've transformed the neighborhood on Halloween, you've taken care of us and each other during a global pandemic. In short, you bought in. You've made it fun and a village and enriched our lives beyond measure. We really are the lucky ones.

ABOUT THE AUTHORS

Chris (MDiv, Covenant Seminary) and Elizabeth live in Columbia, Missouri with their four daughters and a Pomeranian. They work for Cru City and serve as associate staff at their church, The Crossing. They write, speak, and are passionate about helping people love their next-door neighbors.

For additional resources on neighboring:
Placedforapurpose.com

ABOUT GOSPEL-CENTERED DISCIPLESHIP

You may have noticed that there are a lot of resources available for theological education, church planting, and missional church, but not for discipleship. We noticed too, so we started Gospel-Centered Discipleship to address the need for reliable resources on a whole range of discipleship issues.

When we use the term "gospel-centered," we aren't trying to divide Christians into camps, but to promote a way of following Jesus that is centered on the gospel of grace. While all disciples of Jesus believe the gospel is central to Christianity, we often live as if religious rules or spiritual license actually form the center of discipleship.

Jesus calls us to displace those things and replace them with the gospel. We're meant to apply the benefits of the gospel to our lives every day, not to merely bank on them for a single instance of "being saved." A gospel-centered disciple returns to the gospel over and over again, to receive, apply, and spread God's forgiveness and grace into every aspect of life.

GOSPEL-CENTERED DISCIPLESHIP
RESOURCES

Visit GCDiscipleship.com/Books.

Identity is a hot topic these days, and many books have been written on it from a Christian perspective. However, virtually all of them begin in the present and move to the future. Almost none address the earliest chapters of your story where your identity took root. If much of the story you are writing is shaped by the story that was written for you, it makes sense to revisit your past in order to change unhelpful patterns of thought and behavior.

Tracing the Thread: Examining the Story of Self for Lasting Change will guide you back to the three chapters in your story which had the greatest bearing on identity formation—the love you received, the tribes you belonged to, and the voices you listened to—and help you uncover foundational errors in your identity beliefs.

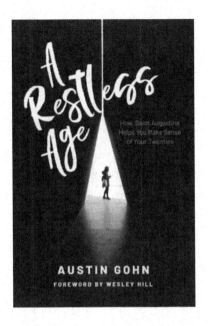

Do your twenties feel restless? You're not the first young adult to feel this way. Saint Augustine describes the same struggle in his Confessions, the most-read spiritual memoir in history. He experimented with different religious options, tried to break destructive habits, struggled to find the right friends, experienced a devastating breakup, and nearly burned out in his career—all before his thirty-second birthday. He spent his twenties looking for rest in all the wrong places.

In *A Restless Age*, Austin Gohn wades through Augustine's *Confessions* to show us how the five searches of young adulthood—answers, habits, belonging, love, and work—are actually searches for rest. "Our heart is restless," Augustine writes, "until it finds rest in you."

The Christian life is knowing God. It is not an impersonal knowledge of bare facts but one rooted in wonder at "the light of the knowledge of the glory of God in the face of Jesus Christ" (2 Cor. 4:6). It is knowing that basks in the glories of the gospel.

In *Gospel Glories from A to Z*, Kelly Havrilla works to reflect some of that glory onto each page as she connects deep biblical truths through the structure of the alphabet. Useful for both those new to the beauty of Christianity and those looking for a fresh way to grow deeper this book aims to make God's grace abundantly clear and accessible. Our hope is that this reflection will spark a desire to venture into deeper waves of gospel glories.

After fifteen plus years of vocational ministry, Ben Connelly had an epiphany. He had missed the great commission. He was really good at keeping Christians happy and really bad at making disciples. *A Pastor's Guide to Everyday Mission* helps those in paid ministry positions rediscover—and live—their life as God's missionaries, even as they minister to God's people.

Too often we limit the power of the gospel to its blessings for us in the afterlife. We fail to see how the power of God, which raised Jesus from the dead, fuels our day-to-day battle against sin in this life. *Renew* shows us the grace of God is able to change us now.

For those looking to break specific sinful habits and temptations as well as those looking to gain a better grasp of how a Christian grows, *Renew* speaks to the power of the gospel today.

ENDNOTES

Foreword

1 Christine D. Pohl, *Making Room: Recovering Hospitality as a Christian Tradition* (Grand Rapids, MI: Eerdmans, 1999), 105–106.

Lesson One

1 Genesis 2:18 (ESV).

2 Genesis 2:17, Romans 6 (ESV).

3 Diana Rab, "The Dilemma of Loneliness," Psychology Today, Aug 27, 2018, https://www.psychologytoday.com/gb/blog /the-empowerment-diary/201808/the-dilemma-loneliness.

4 Jenny Stevens, "The Friend Effect: Why the Secret of Health and Happiness is Surprisingly Simple," *The Guardian*, May 23, 2018, https://www.theguardian.com/society/2018/may/23/the-friend-effect-why-the-secret-of-health-and-happiness-is-surprisingly-simple.

5 Ceylan Yeginsu, "U.K. Appoints A Minister of Loneliness," *The New York Times*, Jan, 17, 2018, https://www.nytimes.com/2018/01/17/world/europe/uk-britain-loneliness.html.

6 Ibid.

7 Luke 10:9b (ESV).

8 Acts 17:26–27 (NIV)

9 Rosaria Butterfield, *The Gospel Comes with a House Key* (Wheaton, IL: Crossway, 2018), 65

10 Matthew 6:10 (NKJV)

11 Acts 17:26–27 (NIV)

12 Rosaria Butterfield, *The Gospel Comes with a House Key* (Wheaton, IL: Crossway, 2018), 65.

Lesson Two

[1] Eli Saslow, "It Was My Job To Find Him," *Washington Post*, June 4, 2018, https://www.washingtonpost.com/ national/it-was-my-job-and-i-didnt-find-him-stoneman-douglas-resource-officer-remains-haunted-by-massacre/2018/06/04/796f1c16–679d-11e8–9e38–24e693b38637_story.

[2] Luke 10:25–28 (ESV).

[3] Luke 10:29 (ESV), emphasis added.

[4] David E. Garland, *Luke*, ed., Clinton E. Arnold, Zondervan Exegetical Commentary on the New Testament Series, Accordance electronic ed. (Grand Rapids, MI: Zondervan, 2011), 439.

[5] Luke 10:36–37 (ESV)

[6] John Newton, "The Good Samaritan."

[7] David E. Garland, *Luke*, ed., Clinton E. Arnold, Zondervan Exegetical Commentary on the New Testament Series, Accordance electronic ed. (Grand Rapids, MI: Zondervan, 2011), 439.

Lesson Three

[1] *Mr. Rogers' Neighborhood*, episode 1478, "Divorce," directed by Hugh Martin, written by Fred Rogers, WQED Studios, 1981.

[2] Some reference Matthew 8:20 "And Jesus said to him, 'Foxes have holes, and birds of the air have nests, but the Son of Man has nowhere to lay his head'" to argue that Jesus was homeless during his ministry. Though it's clear Jesus moved around a lot during this time, we offer that Jesus was probably speaking in hyperbole here; though there could have been times he slept on the side of the road, we think these verses offer enough support to show that Jesus stayed in homes and thought of Capernaum as a home base. See also John 1:38–39.

[3] Mark 2:3 (ESV).

[4] Mark 5:22–23 (ESV).

[5] Matthew 9:36 (ESV), emphasis added.

[6] Amy Julia Becker, "Perfectly Human: We Are All Glorious Ruins by Mary Frances Giles," *Christianity Today*, May 25, 2011, https://www.christianitytoday.com/amyjuliabecker/2011/may/p erfectly-human-we-are-all-glorious-ruins-by-mary-frances.html.

[7] Tim Keller, *Meaning of Marriage* (New York, NY: Penguin Group, 2011), 95.

[8] This idea was influenced by the concepts in Doug Palmeter's book *Grace and Truth Relationship: Finding Authenticity with God and Others* (Lulu.com, 2016).

Lesson Four

[1] Genesis 12:1–3 (ESV).

[2] Metro Goldwyn Mayer ; Act III Communications ; directed by Rob Reiner ; screenplay by William Goldman ; produced by Andrew Scheinman and Rob Reiner. *The Princess Bride*. Santa Monica, CA :*MGM Home Entertainment*, 2000.

[3] Psalm 23:5 (ESV).

[4] Ephesians 2:12–13 (ESV).

[5] Leviticus 19:33 (ESV).

[6] Exodus. 23:9 (ESV).

[7] These thoughts are shaped and influenced by Christine Pohl in her book, *Making Room: Recovering Hospitality as a Christian Tradition* (Grand Rapids, MI: Eerdmans, 1999).

[8] Matt Chandler, "Hospitality and the Greatest Story Ever Told," *The Village Church*, Sermon, June 19, 2016, https://www.tvcresources.net/resource-library/sermons/hospitality-and-the-greatest-story-ever-told/.

[9] Dustin Willis and Brandon Clements, *The Simplest Way to Change the World* (Chicago, IL: Moody Publishers, 2017), 42.

[10] John 15:15 (ESV).

[11] These thoughts were influenced by Dave Cover, "God Has a Name," *The Crossing*, sermon, https://www.thecrossingchurch.com/media-feeds/god-has-a-name/.

[12] Exodus 3:13 (ESV).

[13] Exodus 3:14–15 (ESV).

[14] The Hebrew word YHWH, probably pronounced Yahweh, is most commonly translated LORD but literally means "I AM."

[15] Henri Nouwen, *Reaching Out* (New York, NY: Image Books, 1966), 71.

[16] Dave Runyon and Jay Pavlok, *Art of Neighboring* (Grand Rapids, MI: Baker Books, 2012), 120.

[17] Jeremiah 29:4–7 (ESV).

[18] Henri Nouwen, *Reaching Out* (New York, NY: Image Books, 1966), 71.

Lesson Five

[1] Many of these thoughts come from the influence of Zack Eswine's book *The Imperfect Pastor* (Wheaton, IL: Crossway, 2015). Though it's a book written to pastors, it has some incredibly broad implications and we highly recommend it.

[2] 1 Corinthians 3:5–9 (ESV).

[3] Tim Downs, *Finding Common Ground* (Chicago, IL: Moody Publishers, 1999), 12.

[4] Erik Swanson and Sam Williams, *To Transform a City* (Grand Rapids, MI: Zondervan, 2010), 58.

[5] John Stott, *Christian Mission in the Modern World* (Downers Grove, IL: IVP Books, 2009), 47–48.

[6] Mark 4:30–32 (ESV).

Lesson Six

[1] Tobin Grant, "The Great Decline: 60 Years of Religion in One Graph," *Religion News*, Jan 27, 2014, https://religionnews.com/2014/01/27/great-decline-religion-united-states-one-graph/.

[2] Gregory Smith et al., "In U.S., Decline of Christianity Continues at Rapid Pace," *Pew Research Center*, Oct 17, 2019, https://www.pewforum.org/wp-content/uploads/sites/7/2019/10/Trends-in-Religious-Identity-and-Attendance-FOR-WEB-1.pdf.

[3] Tim Keller, *Center Church* (Grand Rapids, MI: Zondervan, 2012), 281.

[4] 1 Corinthians 3:6–7 (ESV).

[5] Romans 10:17 (ESV).

[6] Tom Goodwin, Cru City Research Project, 2017.

[7] Mark 10:21 (ESV).

[8] David W. Augsburger, *Caring Enough to Hear and Be Heard* (Grand Rapids, MI: Baker Publishers, 1982), 12.

[9] Jonathan Chatraw, quoted in Sarah Eekhoff Zylstra, "Ask And You Shall Evangelize," *The Gospel Coalition*, Nov 14, 2018, https://www.thegospelcoalition.org/article/ask-shall-evangelize/.

[10] Jerram Barrs, *Learning Evangelism from Jesus* (Wheaton, IL: Crossway, 2009), 78.

[11] Eugene Peterson, "A Conversation with Eugene Peterson," interview by Michael John Cusick, *The Mars Hill Review 3*, no. 3, (Fall 1995): 73–90, https://restoringthesoul.com/wp-content/uploads/2018/11/A-Conversation-With-Eugene-Peterson_-pdf.pdf.

[12] Ibid.

[13] C. S. Lewis, *God in the Dock* (Grand Rapids, MI: Eerdmans, 1970), 93.

[14] Luke 18:23–27 (ESV).

[15] Jerram Barrs, *Learning Evangelism from Jesus* (Wheaton, IL: Crossway, 2009), 76.

[16] Luke 18:27 (ESV)

[17] Tom Goodwin, Cru City Research Project, 2017.

[18] Jonathan Chatraw, quoted in Sarah Eekhoff Zylstra, "Ask And You Shall Evangelize," The Gospel Coalition, Nov 14, 2018, https://www.thegospelcoalition.org/article/ask-shall-evangelize/.

[19] Eugene Peterson, "A Conversation with Eugene Peterson," interview by Michael John Cusick, *The Mars Hill Review 3*, no. 3, (Fall 1995): 73–90, https://restoringthesoul.com/wp-content/uploads/2018/11/A-Conversation-With-Eugene-Peterson-pdf.pdf.

Made in USA - North Chelmsford, MA
1176353_9780578736488
12.28.2021 1245